# Should Juveniles Be Tried as Adults?

Hal Marcovitz

**IN**CONTROVERSY

ReferencePoint Press®

San Diego, CA

© 2012 ReferencePoint Press, Inc.
Printed in the United States

**For more information, contact:**
ReferencePoint Press, Inc.
PO Box 27779
San Diego, CA 92198
www.ReferencePointPress.com

LIBRARY OF CONGRESS CATALOGING-IN-PUBLICATION DATA

Marcovitz, Hal.
  Should juveniles be tried as adults? / By Hal Marcovitz.
    p. cm. -- (In controversy)
  Includes bibliographical references and index.
  ISBN-13: 978-1-60152-230-6 (hardback)
  ISBN-10: 1-60152-230-4 (hardback)
  1. Juvenile delinquents--United States--Juvenile literature. 2. Sentences (Criminal procedure)--United States--Juvenile literature. 3. Prosecution--United States--Juvenile literature. I. Title.
  KF9795.M37 2012
  345.73'04--dc23
                                                                                          2011030334

# Contents

# Foreword

I n 2008, as the US economy and economies worldwide were falling into the worst recession since the Great Depression, most Americans had difficulty comprehending the complexity, magnitude, and scope of what was happening. As is often the case with a complex, controversial issue such as this historic global economic recession, looking at the problem as a whole can be overwhelming and often does not lead to understanding. One way to better comprehend such a large issue or event is to break it into smaller parts. The intricacies of global economic recession may be difficult to understand, but one can gain insight by instead beginning with an individual contributing factor, such as the real estate market. When examined through a narrower lens, complex issues become clearer and easier to evaluate.

This is the idea behind ReferencePoint Press's *In Controversy* series. The series examines the complex, controversial issues of the day by breaking them into smaller pieces. Rather than looking at the stem cell research debate as a whole, a title would examine an important aspect of the debate such as *Is Stem Cell Research Necessary?* or *Is Embryonic Stem Cell Research Ethical?* By studying the central issues of the debate individually, researchers gain a more solid and focused understanding of the topic as a whole.

Each book in the series provides a clear, insightful discussion of the issues, integrating facts and a variety of contrasting opinions for a solid, balanced perspective. Personal accounts and direct quotes from academic and professional experts, advocacy groups, politicians, and others enhance the narrative. Sidebars add depth to the discussion by expanding on important ideas and events. For quick reference, a list of key facts concludes every chapter. Source notes, an annotated organizations list, bibliography, and index provide student researchers with additional tools for papers and class discussion.

The *In Controversy* series also challenges students to think critically about issues, to improve their problem-solving skills, and to sharpen their ability to form educated opinions. As President Barack Obama stated in a March 2009 speech, success in the twenty-first century will not be measurable merely by students' ability to "fill in a bubble on a test but whether they possess 21st century skills like problem-solving and critical thinking and entrepreneurship and creativity." Those who possess these skills will have a strong foundation for whatever lies ahead.

No one can know for certain what sort of world awaits today's students. What we can assume, however, is that those who are inquisitive about a wide range of issues; open-minded to divergent views; aware of bias and opinion; and able to reason, reflect, and reconsider will be best prepared for the future. As the international development organization Oxfam notes, "Today's young people will grow up to be the citizens of the future: but what that future holds for them is uncertain. We can be quite confident, however, that they will be faced with decisions about a wide range of issues on which people have differing, contradictory views. If they are to develop as global citizens all young people should have the opportunity to engage with these controversial issues."

*In Controversy* helps today's students better prepare for tomorrow. An understanding of the complex issues that drive our world and the ability to think critically about them are essential components of contributing, competing, and succeeding in the twenty-first century.

# When Young People Face Life in Prison

Zong Vang, a 13-year-old boy from Green Bay, Wisconsin, died in a manner that was both senseless and horrific. Vang had been sent to a grocery store by his parents to buy tomatoes. On the way home he was accosted by five youths who knocked him off his bicycle, then chased him into a parking garage. After cornering the boy on the top floor of the garage, two of the youths, Omer Ninham, 14, and Richard Crapeau, 13, seized Vang by his wrists and ankles, then flung him over the side. Vang fell five stories to his death.

Vang was a random target. None of the boys implicated in the attack knew him. The court dealt harshly with the attackers: Charged with Vang's murder in adult court, Ninham and Crapeau were convicted and sentenced to life in prison. In Crapeau's case, the judge ruled that he could not apply for parole until he served at least 50 years in prison. Ninham received an even harsher sentence—the judge ruled that he must serve life in prison without possibility of parole.

## Harsh Sentences Common for Adults

The murder of Vang occurred in 1998. Following the sentencing of Ninham, his lawyers appealed the harshness of the penalty, arguing that it is wrong to sentence a defendant convicted of a crime at the age of 14 to life in prison without parole. By 2011 the lengthy appeals process had finally found its way to the Wisconsin Supreme Court.

Ninham's lawyers argued that sentencing the boy to life without parole violates the US constitutional provision against cruel and unusual punishment. The Wisconsin Supreme Court disagreed with that assertion, finding that the sentence imposed on Ninham was appropriate. "Contemporary society views the punishment as proportionate to the offense,"[1] writes Wisconsin Supreme Court Justice Annette Kingsland Ziegler.

The harsh sentences imposed on Ninham and Crapeau are common among adults who commit murder and similarly heinous offenses, but Ninham and Crapeau were juveniles at the time of the crime. For more than a century, most juvenile offenders have been treated differently by legislatures and the courts, which have found that young people have a limited degree of responsibility for their actions. Youthful offenders have been largely tried under different rules in courts established specifically to hear juvenile cases. For example, sentences handed down in juvenile courts are typically much lighter—even in homicide cases. Moreover, the sentences are usually tailored to rehabilitate rather than to punish the young offenders. According to a 2005 report by the advocacy group Human Rights Watch:

> *"Contemporary society views the punishment [of Omer Ninham] as proportionate to the offense."*[1]
>
> — Wisconsin Supreme Court Justice Annette Kingsland Ziegler.

> The terrible crimes committed by children can ruin lives, causing injury and death to the victims and grief to their families and friends. Sentencing must reflect the seriousness of the crime, but it also must acknowledge that culpability can be substantially diminished by reason of the youth and immaturity of the perpetrator. Child offenders should be given the possibility of freedom one day, when they have matured and demonstrated their remorse and capacity for rehabilitation.[2]

## Paying the Penalty

Many members of the public would seem to agree. According to a 2010 report by the advocacy group National Juvenile Justice Network, which supports rehabilitative efforts for young offenders,

*Youth offenders complete a language arts assignment at an Idaho juvenile detention center school. Juveniles who are tried as adults receive much harsher sentences than young offenders who go through the juvenile court system, where the focus is rehabilitation.*

polling shows that 89 percent of people believe "almost all youth who commit crimes have the potential to change," while more than 70 percent agree that "incarcerating youthful offenders without rehabilitation is the same as giving up on them."[3]

However, many other advocates call for harsh sentences on juvenile offenders, arguing that lawbreakers—regardless of their ages—deserve to be behind bars. A statement by the National Organization of Victims of Juvenile Lifers says, "People who intentionally and brutally kill people should go to prison, sometimes for the rest of their lives. Most are extremely dangerous. . . . Some of them have lost the right to walk among us. Society has a right to be safe."[4]

In recent years lawmakers have responded to these demands. In many state capitals, legislators have written measures that treat young offenders more like their adult counterparts. As a result of these measures, many cases that were formerly tried in juvenile courts are now tried in the same courtrooms where adult criminals face justice. When they arrive in court, juveniles learn they must stand trial under the same rules that adults face—and if they are convicted, they face the same type of lengthy and punitive sentences typically administered to adult defendants.

## Reversing the Trend

Juvenile defense advocates believe such harsh treatment of young offenders does not serve as a deterrent to crime, nor does it help rehabilitate the offenders. They believe the trend should be reversed and the courts should return to treating all young offenders under the specific rules established for juvenile courts. Says Shay Bilchik, director of the Center for Juvenile Justice Reform at Georgetown University in Washington, DC, "[The] principles [of] separating delinquent juveniles from hardened criminals, treating youth as developmentally different from adults, and viewing young people as being inherently malleable and subject to positive change in a rehabilitative setting are still fundamentally sound."[5]

In Ninham's case, he is represented by attorneys for the Equal Justice Initiative, a Montgomery, Alabama, organization dedicated to returning juvenile cases to juvenile courts. Following the ruling by the Wisconsin Supreme Court, Byron Stevenson, the Equal Justice Initiative lawyer who represents Ninham, said he intends to take his client's case to the US Supreme Court. He says, "I absolutely believe it's just a matter of time before states are going to have to re-evaluate the judgment that you can punish [a juvenile] the same way you can punish an adult."[6]

As his appeals continue to crawl through the courts, Ninham has no choice but to sit in his prison cell and pay the penalty for the murder of a defenseless 13-year-old victim. Unless his attorneys can overturn the law, Ninham will have no opportunity to win parole and will instead spend the rest of his life behind bars, a sentence that a judge has determined to be an appropriate punishment for the crime Ninham committed as a child.

> "I absolutely believe it's just a matter of time before states are going to have to re-evaluate the judgment that you can punish [a juvenile] the same way you can punish an adult."[6]
>
> — Byron Stevenson, attorney for Omer Ninham.

## Facts

- The advocacy group Equal Justice Initiative reported in 2011 that more than 2,200 Americans have been sentenced to life in prison without parole for crimes they committed at age 17 or younger.

- According to the Center for Juvenile Justice Reform at Georgetown University, about 200,000 defendants under the age of 18 are tried in US adult courts each year.

- The National Organization of Victims of Juvenile Lifers reports that 12 percent of all juveniles serving prison sentences of life without parole were 15 years old or younger at the time they committed their crimes.

# What Are the Roots of the Juvenile Offender Controversy?

I n the long history of American jurisprudence, the trial and sentencing of Gerry Gault of Gila County, Arizona, stands out as a landmark case that helped establish the rights of juvenile defendants. However, the Gault case also surfaces as an important milestone in the movement to treat juvenile offenders under the same rules established for adult criminal defendants.

Gault was 15 years old in 1964 when he made an indecent phone call to a neighbor. The neighbor called police who responded quickly, taking Gault into custody. The boy was home alone at the time. Police made no attempt to call his parents or otherwise contact them after his arrest.

Gault soon appeared before a judge in Gila County juvenile court. After a brief hearing the boy was sentenced to a state juvenile detention center until his twenty-first birthday. At the hearing he was denied representation by a lawyer. Moreover, Gault's parents received no notice of the hearing. No witnesses were called to testify against Gault—not even the neighbor who received the lewd phone call.

While it may seem as though Gault was railroaded off to prison, that was not the case. In fact, authorities treated Gault within the confines of Arizona law as it existed at the time. The state's legislature had given widespread discretion to juvenile court judges, providing them with enormous authority over the lives of the youthful offenders who appeared before them. The issue in the case was not whether Gault had been mistreated by Arizona police and court officials but whether the law in Arizona should have permitted them so much authority over his life. Says David N. Sandberg, a Boston University law professor and expert on juvenile justice, "Gault's 'sentence' was bad enough, but the process by which it was arrived at was worse."[7]

## Kangaroo Court

An attorney retained by Gault's parents appealed the sentence, contending that Gault had been denied due process of law guaranteed by the US Constitution. Indeed, the Constitution mandates that defendants be tried in public courtrooms, that they be represented by attorneys, and that they have the right to face their accusers. Gault's attorney also contended that the punishment— six years in a juvenile detention center—was cruel and unusual. The lawyer pointed out that if Gault had been convicted in adult court, the maximum penalty for an obscene phone call was a $50 fine and two months in prison.

The case was eventually heard by the US Supreme Court, which in 1967 overturned Gault's conviction, finding that Arizona's juvenile court system denied young defendants due process of law. "Under our constitution," wrote Justice Abe Fortas, "the condition of being a boy does not justify a kangaroo court."[8]

However, the nine-member court's decision was not unanimous—Justice Potter Stewart cast the lone vote against overturning the conviction. Stewart said he was concerned that by granting juvenile defendants the same rights as adult defendants, they would likely also be tried as adults and face similar punishments as those leveled against adult defendants. He feared that American justice would take a step back to the era when young children accused of crimes found themselves standing in courtrooms alongside adult killers, thieves, sex offend-

*"Under our constitution the condition of being a boy does not justify a kangaroo court."[8]*

— US Supreme Court Justice Abe Fortas.

## A Juvenile Offender's Path Through the Courts

From the moment of arrest a juvenile faces a far different path through the courts than an adult would experience. For starters, an adult who is arrested may have to post bail. If the defendant cannot make bail, he or she will sit in jail until trial. A juvenile who is arrested cannot be expected to raise bail—which could total many thousands of dollars. Instead, the judge may release the juvenile into the custody of his or her parents or immediately order detention in a juvenile detention facility.

Meanwhile, the prosecutor will file either a delinquency petition with the court, asking for trial in juvenile court, or a waiver petition, asking for the case to be transferred into adult court. If the defendant is to be tried in adult court, the Constitution guarantees the right to a speedy trial. Most states have adopted the so-called 180-day rule, which mandates that criminal trials must commence within six months of a defendant's arrest. In practice, due to crowded court calendars, most defendants find themselves walking into courtrooms very close to their 180-day limits.

In contrast, most juvenile court hearings are held within a few weeks of the arrest. These hearings are known as adjudication hearings, during which the prosecutor will present evidence about the crime as well as testimony from social workers, psychologists, and others. If the judge determines the juvenile did commit the crime, a verdict of delinquency will be rendered.

ers, and other hardened criminals. Writes Stewart, "To impose the court's long catalog of requirements upon juvenile proceedings in every area of the country is to invite a long step backwards into the nineteenth century. In that era there were no juvenile proceedings, and a child was tried in a conventional criminal court with all the trappings of a conventional criminal trial."[9]

## Treated as Adults

During the early years of the nineteenth century, the laws in America were still relatively young and subject to few interpretations by the Supreme Court. Although the framers of the US Constitution had established certain rights for criminal defendants, when it came to juvenile offenders the law treated them similarly to how they had been treated in England and other European countries. Young defendants were subjected to trials in adult courts, as well as harsh penalties following their convictions, because for centuries the law saw no difference between a young criminal and an adult criminal. In the eyes of the law, a criminal was a criminal.

When a group of criminals was marched in front of a judge, all chained together, a young lawbreaker could expect no special treatment. In English author Charles Dickens's 1838 novel *Oliver Twist*, readers are introduced to the character Jack Dawkins. Also known as the Artful Dodger, Dawkins is the youthful leader of a gang of young pickpockets. At the end of the novel Oliver is saved from a life of crime by a long-lost relative, but the Dodger suffers a far different fate: He is arrested, tried in adult court, and—for the crime of stealing a silver snuff box—sentenced to a penal colony in Australia. The characters in *Oliver Twist* are fictitious, but literary scholars believe Dickens based them on real-life London street waifs of the era and the fates that awaited them should they be caught and put on trial. Says Michael P. Brown, professor of criminal justice at Ball State University in Indiana, "The criminal sanctioning of juvenile offenders is not a contemporary phenomenon. Juveniles have been punished as adults for centuries."[10]

Indeed, in Europe as well as in colonial America, by the age of five most children were believed old enough to work in the family's farm fields or learn trades as apprentices; therefore, young people were regarded as adults. And when they broke the law, they were put on trial as though they were adults.

> "To impose the Court's long catalog of requirements upon juvenile proceedings in every area of the country is to invite a long step backwards into the nineteenth century."[9]
>
> — US Supreme Court Justice Potter Stewart.

## Era of Reforms

Even as readers pored through *Oliver Twist*, reforms were under way that would lead to significant changes in the treatment of young offenders. By the end of the seventeenth century, church and community leaders in England and other European countries promoted the notion that children are weak and innocent and need guidance from adults. Schooling became mandatory, at least for a few years of a child's life. In the eighteenth century, those principles were adopted by the American colonies and, following the War of Independence, by the new state governments.

Meanwhile, other reforms were under way. During the 1800s, many state governments opened juvenile detention facilities specifically to house young offenders, thus separating them from older inmates who were likely to abuse them—both physically and sexually. Moreover, reformers realized that young people housed in adult prisons were also likely to learn how to be better criminals from their adult tutors. The first detention facility intended specifically for young offenders was the New York House of Refuge, which opened in 1825.

Soon, political leaders embraced the concept that juvenile centers should be more than just prisons. In 1855 the Chicago Reform School opened, becoming one of the first facilities to house young offenders and provide them with an education. Certainly, reform school could be an unpleasant place to spend one's childhood, but at least the young offenders were among people their own age, and their teachers were professional educators rather than older convicts. Many of the schools taught trades, farm work, and other skills that the young people could use upon their release and which, hopefully, would help make them productive citizens rather than repeat offenders. Even more liberal attitudes were on the horizon: In 1917 a Catholic priest, Edward J. Flanagan, established Boys Town near Omaha, Nebraska, which emphasized intervention and rehabilitation rather than punishment in its treatment of youthful offenders.

*"The criminal sanctioning of juvenile offenders is not a contemporary phenomenon. Juveniles have been punished as adults for centuries."*[10]

— Michael P. Brown, professor of criminal justice at Ball State University in Indiana.

## Informal and Nonadversarial

Another significant reform occurred in the courtrooms themselves. In 1899 the first courtroom designated specifically to hear juvenile cases convened in Chicago. By 1925 most states had adopted the concept and established their own juvenile courts.

The rules for juvenile courts would evolve—particularly after the Gault decision established the rights of young offenders. Still, in most juvenile courts that are in operation today, young offenders discover a far different environment than they may find in adult courtrooms.

For starters, most states bar public access to juvenile court records. This means a former juvenile court defendant usually does not have to disclose a criminal record to a prospective employer. In contrast, most adult court records are open to public inspection; if a job applicant claims no prior record of arrest or conviction, the potential employer can verify whether this is true. Certainly, many employers are hesitant to hire anybody they know to have been involved in criminal activities—even if those job applicants have told the truth about themselves and paid their penalties.

Another significant difference between juvenile court and adult court is that in adult court the defendant has a right to a trial by jury, while in juvenile court the judge is the sole decider of the truth. Although the Gault case established that the defendant had been denied certain rights guaranteed under the Constitution, a subsequent case decided by the US Supreme Court found that granting trials by juries in juvenile proceedings would completely erase any significant difference between juvenile courts and adult courts. In a 1971 case Justice Byron White wrote, "Compelling a jury trial might remake the proceeding into a fully adversary process, and effectively end the idealistic prospect of an intimate, informal protective proceeding."[11]

White's comments were rooted in the legal concept known as *parens patriae*, a Latin term that means "parent of the country." Essentially, the juvenile court had taken over the role of parent, deciding what would be best for the defendant.

Moreover, from the earliest days of their existence, juvenile court proceedings were intended to be informal and nonadversarial. In some counties, juvenile court judges do not sit on the bench, looking down on the young people brought before them, but at tables across from the offenders in a manner that is regarded as far less intimidating. The ultimate goal is not only to determine the guilt or innocence of the defendant but to find out

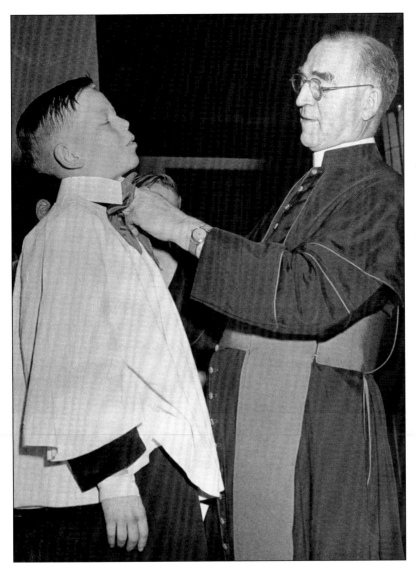

*Edward J. Flanagan, the Catholic priest who established Boys Town in Nebraska in 1917, helps one of his young charges prepare for a choir performance in the 1940s. Flanagan's program for juvenile offenders emphasized intervention and rehabilitation over punishment.*

why the young person committed the crime and to determine the best mode of rehabilitation. Among the questions the court attempts to answer are: What is his or her home life like? How does the defendant perform in school? Has there been abuse in the child's life?

## Rehabilitation Rather than Punishment

After serving as a fact finder and concluding that the defendant committed the crime, rather than finding the offender "guilty" the

# Father Flanagan's Boys Town

The reform movement in juvenile justice took a step forward in 1917 when a Catholic priest, Edward J. Flanagan, established Boys Town in Nebraska as a home and school for juvenile offenders, as well as orphans and other homeless young people, all male. Flanagan believed young offenders should be rehabilitated rather than punished. "Our young people are our greatest wealth," he said. "Give them a chance and they will give a good account of themselves. No boy wants to be bad. There is only bad environment, bad training, bad example, bad thinking."

Among the first five residents to what was originally known as Boys' Home were three boys referred by juvenile court and two homeless boys. For years the students were housed in dormitories, but in the 1970s the school changed its residential program so that students share the homes of nearby families, in the belief that many young offenders lack supportive family environments.

A major part of the Boys Town program is based on the philosophy that the students should govern themselves and be responsible for their own decisions: The students elect their own government, including a mayor and council. Today, more than 300 students, including girls, are enrolled at the Boys Town campus near Omaha.

Quoted in Nebraska State Historical Society, "Father Flanagan's Boys' Home," June 4, 2004. www.nebraskahistory.org.

judge will render a verdict of "delinquency." As for the sentence, the judge's decision on what to do with the defendant will be focused more on rehabilitation than on punishment. "[The court] would serve as the benevolent parent—all knowing and all-loving, wanting only that which is in the best interest of the children," says Brown. "Consequently, instead of harsh, punitive sanctions that sought to deter, the court would seek long-term behavioral change by providing guidance to youths so woefully lacking from their natural parents. Sentences were to be customized to meet the needs of each juvenile so as to optimize the rehabilitative effects of court intervention."[12]

Judges who preside over adult cases often have few discretionary powers when it comes to sentencing. Most laws are clear on the length and punitive nature of sentences, depending on the severity of the crime and the record of the defendant—that is, whether he or she is a repeat offender. Sentences can range from probation—in which the defendant remains free during the course of his or her sentence—to very long prison terms.

On the other hand, most state laws empower judges with wide measures of discretion when it comes to sentencing juvenile offenders. Among the options a judge can select are probation, counseling, community service, detention in a juvenile facility, and restitution to the victims. The bottom line is that in many states the law permits the juvenile court judge to tailor a sentence that best enables the young offender to rehabilitate and start fresh. Says Thomas Edwards, former presiding judge of the juvenile court of Santa Clara County, California:

> A 14-year-old is still growing, may not appreciate the consequences of [criminal] behavior, and is susceptible to change, at least to a higher degree than a 24-year-old is. . . . I think we have a real shot at trying to straighten out the 14-year-old, and even the people who are a little bit hard-nosed in the system, such as your average prosecutor, will sometimes grudgingly admit that, with a 14-year-old, given the proper level of accountability and the proper types of programs to change their behavior, we have a chance at salvaging these kids.
>
> But with a 24-year-old, I think the whole consensus of opinion is, "You've had your chance, you're now an adult, you've made a bad decision, you've hurt somebody, you've done it. Now you pay the price."[13]

# Rising Juvenile Crime Rate

All of these reforms were made with good intentions, but by the 1950s law enforcement officials and political leaders felt they had to respond to a rising rate of juvenile crime. Legal experts attributed the problem to the growth of inner-city youth gangs, a trend that was dramatized and even glorified in such popular films of the era as *Rebel Without a Cause*, *Blackboard Jungle*, and *West Side Story*. Many parents, as well as police and prosecutors, blamed rock-and-roll music for fostering juvenile delinquency. These fears may have been stoked when the hit song "Rock Around the Clock," which became an early anthem of the rock-and-roll generation, was played during the opening credits of *Blackboard Jungle*. The film told the story of disruptive delinquents at an American high school whose antics were punctuated by Bill Haley's song, whose simple lyrics urged teens to devote themselves not to studying or preparing for their careers but to music, dancing, and good times.

> "With a 14-year-old, given the proper level of accountability and the proper types of programs to change their behavior, we have a chance at salvaging these kids."[13]
>
> — Thomas Edwards, former presiding judge of the juvenile court of Santa Clara County, California.

Police cracked down on juvenile crime during the 1950s. Nationally, the number of juvenile arrests doubled between 1948 and 1957. In New York City, where juvenile gangs were particularly common, the arrest rate among young people tripled from 1950 to 1959.

The crackdown would not produce the desired effect: The influx of arrests did little more than overwhelm the juvenile justice system. Juvenile detention facilities became overcrowded while the ability of social workers to provide rehabilitative programs was severely taxed. During the 1960s, an era of great social reform in America, civil libertarians complained that young offenders were being warehoused in juvenile institutions that were not terribly different from adult prisons. Acting on these concerns, Congress passed the 1974 Juvenile Justice and Delinquency Prevention Act, which provided grants for states to develop community-based programs for rehabilitating young offenders as alternatives to institutionalization. A 1980 amendment to the act contained an important provision: It mandated that inmates under the age of

18 could not be housed in the same facilities that house adult inmates. Although the amendment left room for some exceptions, it meant that in most cases, states that wanted to prosecute young people as adults would have to build separate facilities to house them after conviction and sentencing.

*A 16-year-old boy (back to the camera) accused of shooting his mother to death and critically wounding his father attends a hearing in juvenile court. The juvenile court setting, with participants seated around a table, is less intimidating than that of adult courts.*

# Widening Waiver Laws

Still, as crime rates continued to rise in the 1970s and 1980s, many political leaders started taking a far dimmer view of efforts to rehabilitate young offenders. For example, even as reform-minded lawmakers modified juvenile justice statutes to make them less punitive and more rehabilitative, they continued to permit judges, as well as prosecutors, the power to "waive," or transfer, juvenile cases into adult courtrooms. In some cases lawmakers designated specific crimes that would automatically be waived into adult court—usually homicides and other crimes of violence, particularly those involving the use of weapons. These statutes are known as "automatic transfer" or "statutory exclusion" laws. In response to the rising rate of crime among young people, lawmakers looked again at these laws, expanding them to include other crimes as well.

*"At the turn of the [last] century, there was a social reform movement in this country. The creation of juvenile court was a piece of that. We do not live now in a time of social reform."*[14]

— Marsha Levick, legal director of the Philadelphia-based Juvenile Law Center.

According to the Office of Juvenile Justice and Delinquency Prevention in the US Department of Justice, the number of juvenile cases waived into adult court by judges or prosecutors increased from about 7,200 in 1985 to more than 12,000 in 1994. Following the peak year of 1994 the number of juvenile waivers declined to about 8,000 in 2001 and remained steady at that level for the past decade.

The Office of Juvenile Justice and Delinquency Prevention does not believe those statistics reflect a decrease in serious juvenile crime. Rather, the agency suggests that state legislatures have rewritten their laws, disqualifying many crimes from trial in juvenile court. In other words, fewer waivers are permitted by judges and prosecutors not because fewer serious crimes are committed but because state lawmakers want those cases to go *directly* to adult courts. Essentially, they have removed the discretionary powers that judges and prosecutors could employ to determine whether young offenders would be best served in juvenile courts or whether their cases demand the strict rules and potentially punitive punishments that are found in the criminal courts.

# Get-Tough Trend

The trend toward getting tough on juvenile offenders has prompted many activists to suggest that—just as Justice Potter Stewart predicted nearly a half-century ago—the juvenile justice system has taken a step backward to the days when children were tried routinely in adult courtrooms alongside society's most vicious thugs. Says Marsha Levick, legal director of the Philadelphia-based Juvenile Law Center, "At the turn of the [last] century, there was a social reform movement in this country. The creation of juvenile court was a piece of that. We do not live now in a time of social reform. There is not a broad progressive movement sweeping the country."[14]

Still, young people who commit crimes are more likely than not to face justice in the juvenile court system. According to the Office of Juvenile Justice and Delinquency Prevention, nearly 1.7 million cases were heard by juvenile court judges in 2008—the most recent year for which statistics are available. The statistics also indicate, though, that the 2008 juvenile court caseload was larger by nearly a half-million more cases than in 1987. That steady rise in the national juvenile court caseload provides hard evidence that despite the best efforts of both reformers and advocates for get-tough policies, each year more and more young people find themselves in trouble with the law.

## Facts

- Of the nearly 1.7 million crimes prosecuted in juvenile courts in 2008, the largest share—more than 600,000—involved vandalism and theft. Crimes against people—assaults, rapes, and homicides—accounted for more than 400,000. Most of the others involved drug, alcohol, and disorderly conduct cases.

- Since 1992, 49 states have enhanced the powers of prosecutors and judges to transfer juvenile cases to adult courts; the lone state that substantially limits waivers is Nebraska.

- According to the American Bar Association, 29 states have enacted statutory exclusion provisions in their legal codes, listing various offenses, mostly violent, that by law prohibit the cases from being heard in juvenile court.

- The first young offender to be tried in Chicago's juvenile court in 1899 was 11-year-old Henry Campbell, who was charged with theft. The judge found Campbell delinquent and, as a sentence, sent him to live with his grandmother.

- Although juvenile offenders are largely diverted from the adult criminal justice system, all states permit police to fingerprint and photograph the young people they arrest.

- According to the US Department of Justice, 44 states enter the names of juvenile offenders in databases that can be accessed by police who use the information to investigate crimes.

# Are Juveniles Responsible for the Crimes They Commit?

On a winter's day in 2003, 33-year-old Elaine Cowell, the mother of three children, dozed in the front seat of her family's van as her husband drove home after a day of skiing. As the van traveled under an overpass near Allentown, Pennsylvania, an 18-pound chunk of ice dropped onto the car. It smashed through the windshield and struck Cowell in the chest, killing her.

Police soon learned the death was no accident. Their investigation led them to 15-year-old Dennis Gumbs, who had purposely dropped the ice from the overpass. It was a prank—Gumbs simply wanted to see if he could hit one of the cars racing below with a chunk of ice tossed from above. "He feels very bad about the situation," Gumbs's father, Emilio, told reporters shortly after his son's arrest. "He's also thinking of his own life and the outcome now that it's been altered. He's a kid with a big heart. He's feeling it and he's going to feel it for the rest of his life."[15]

Gumbs was charged with murder. Prosecutors intended to try his case in adult court, but the boy's lawyer asked Judge Lawrence J. Brenner to transfer the case to juvenile court. Brenner convened a hearing, and after listening to testimony from mental health experts, the judge concluded the case belonged in juvenile court.

One of the psychiatrists who testified was Dorothy Otnow Lewis, who evaluated Gumbs's mental state prior to the hearing. Lewis concluded that Gumbs was, in many respects, a normal teenager. "He has very poor judgment," the psychiatrist said. "He has very poor impulse control."[16]

A few months later, Gumbs was tried in juvenile court in the death of Cowell. He admitted to tossing the ice chunk from the overpass but said he never realized it could do harm. "I thought it would just crumble when it hit something,"[17] he said. Gumbs was not found guilty of murder but rather judged delinquent by Brenner. The judge sentenced Gumbs to a juvenile detention center until the age of 21. If he had been tried in adult court, his sentence would probably have been much longer, and he would have been forced to serve his time in a state prison.

In 2008 Gumbs turned 21. He was released from juvenile detention and returned home to pick up his life. A few months before his release, the court convened a hearing to evaluate Gumbs's mental health. During the hearing, Gumbs said he understood the nature of his crime and the sorrow he brought to the victim's family. He said, "I want you to see I am not the same person I had been years ago."[18]

## Work in Progress

The question in the Gumbs case is not whether the young defendant knew the difference between right and wrong. Gumbs knew it was wrong to drop the ice onto the cars racing below. Rather, the Gumbs case illustrates how young people very often do not understand the consequences of their actions. Gumbs testified that he did not realize a chunk of ice hurled off a bridge could turn into a deadly weapon. Moreover, the psychiatrist who evaluated Gumbs for the court concluded that, like many teenagers, Gumbs often could not control his impulsive behavior. In other words, when he picked up that chunk of ice and conceived the idea of dropping it onto the cars below, no warning signal went off in his brain alerting him that what he was about to do could harm someone. Says David Fassler, a psychiatry professor at the University of Vermont College of Medicine, "It doesn't mean adolescents can't make a rational decision or appreciate the difference between right and wrong. It does mean, particularly when confronted with stressful or emotional decisions, they are more likely to act impulsively, on instinct, without fully understanding or analyzing the consequences of their actions."[19]

Indeed, when young people commit acts that hurt people or damage property, they may have no malicious intentions—they may simply think it is all a game. In recent years, psychiatrists, physicians, and other researchers have gathered a considerable amount of evidence suggesting that the teenage brain is a work in progress and that young people are often incapable of knowing that what they do may have devastating consequences. And if science suggests teenagers are generally incapable of thinking through the consequences of their decisions, should they be treated as criminals when they hurt people, steal, or damage property?

*Dennis Gumbs, 15, said he did not realize he could kill someone when he dropped a huge chunk of ice off a freeway overpass. Gumbs's action killed Elaine Cowell, pictured with her husband and three children in a family photograph displayed by her father.*

# Age of Criminal Responsibility

The notion that juveniles lack the maturity to intentionally commit criminal acts dates back well before the development of psychology as a science. In the eighteenth century, the authors of the English criminal code concluded that no child under seven is capable of forming a criminal act. These early experts set an important precedent in law when they determined that for an act to be regarded as criminal, three factors must be in place: first, the commission of the crime itself—in Latin, the *actus reus*; second, the *mens rea*, or the intent to commit the crime (*mens rea* means "guilty mind"); and third, the *corpus delicti*—the interaction between the act and the intent to commit it. Therefore, under British law, since youths were considered incapable of forming intent, the mens rea, they were considered legally unable to commit a crime. "Most young children do not have the intelligence, judgment, emotional maturity, and moral capacity to make the rational choices the criminal law requires," write law professors Richard G. Singer and John Q. La Fond. "For this reason, the law does not hold very young children responsible even for behavior designed to cause serious harm."[20]

These principles were adopted by lawmakers in America. However, no national standard declares an exact age at which a defendant is considered capable of knowing that what he or she is planning to do is wrong. The states have adopted a variety of laws declaring the so-called age of criminal responsibility. Thirty-seven states, as well as the District of Columbia and the federal justice system, have set the minimum age of criminal responsibility at 18, meaning that for the most part, defendants 17 and younger are tried in juvenile courts.

As for the states that automatically try defendants younger than 18 in adult court, most have declared the age of criminal responsibility to be 17. A handful of states, including New York, Wisconsin, North Carolina, Massachusetts, and Illinois, regard 16 as the minimum age of criminal responsibility.

"When confronted with stressful or emotional decisions, [adolescents] . . . are more likely to act impulsively, on instinct, without fully understanding or analyzing the consequences of their actions."[19]

— David Fassler, psychiatry professor at the University of Vermont College of Medicine.

Just because these states and other jurisdictions have established minimum ages of criminal responsibility does not mean that they do not try people below those minimum ages in adult court. Many of the laws contain automatic transfer provisions under which cases involving juveniles are sent to adult court. And, of course, in many cases prosecutors and judges can exercise waivers, transferring juveniles to adult court at their discretion.

However, some states have established a minimum age for juveniles tried in adult court—meaning that waivers or automatic transfers for defendants below the minimum age are not permitted. These minimum ages range from as young as 10 in Kansas and Vermont to as old as 15 in New Mexico. In 22 states, no minimum age is set by statute, leaving it up to the discretion of judges and prosecutors to decide when a defendant is old enough to have formed criminal intent.

## The Debate Changes

Many of the laws establishing the age of criminal responsibility have evolved over decades. Typically, state legislators have responded to upward trends in juvenile crime by amending their laws to mandate that younger defendants be tried in adult courts—essentially lowering the age of criminal responsibility. In recent years, though, the debate has changed—instead of enacting legislation to lower the age of criminal responsibility state governments are now assessing proposals to raise the age. Indeed, between 2006 and 2011, legislators in Illinois, Missouri, New York, North Carolina, and Wisconsin all debated bills that would amend their automatic transfer laws to exclude younger defendants, effectively raising the minimum age of criminal responsibility. By 2011 none of those states had taken action. However, in 2010 Connecticut rescinded its automatic transfer law for juveniles 16 and under and in 2012 plans to rescind its transfer law for 17-year-old offenders, meaning that most offenders under 18 will be tried in juvenile court.

Legislators in Connecticut, as well as in the other states where the issue has been debated, have responded to new research that

> *"Most young children do not have the intelligence, judgment, emotional maturity, and moral capacity to make the rational choices the criminal law requires."*[20]
>
> — Law professors Richard G. Singer and John Q. La Fond.

# Pruning Brain Cells

The lack of "white matter" in a teenager's brain may be one reason young people make poor decisions, including those that lead them to commit crimes. Another physiological reason that may get in the way of making good decisions is that teenagers have too much "grey matter."

Grey matter is composed of neurons, which are brain cells. These cells process thoughts and communicate with one another. At age 12, grey matter starts dying off in a process known as "pruning." This is good for the brain because many of these cells serve no purpose. Until the pruning process has been completed, the excess grey matter can get in the way of rational thought. Between the ages of 13 and 18, teenagers are believed to lose 1 percent of grey matter per year.

Moreover, the ages of 13 and 18 are pivotal in the development of the brain because the grey matter that dies off includes cells that are not in use. In other words, if teenagers use the neurons that help them study, those cells survive. If they use the cells that prompt them to commit mischief, those neurons will be saved. Says neuroscientist Jay Giedd, "If a teen is doing music or sports or academics, those are the cells and connections that will be hardwired. If they're lying on the couch or playing video games . . . those are the cells and connections that are going to survive."

Quoted in Sarah Spinks, "Adolescent Brains Are Works in Progress," *Frontline*, January 2002. www.pbs.org.

has emerged, providing scientific evidence that young people may not possess the mental ability to understand that they may be committing crimes. The scientific research indicates that important functions of the brain—including those that control behavior—are still in their formative stages during the teenage years. "Conscience and the ability to develop judgment are not fully developed in adolescents, and this raises real questions about culpability," says Steven J. Berkowitz, a psychiatrist and professor at the Yale University Child Study Center who urged the Connecticut legislature to amend its juvenile crime laws. "As we know, adolescents tend to be more impulsive and more risk taking. They literally do not have the neurological equipment to put on the brakes the way that adults generally do."[21] In Wisconsin, a 2010 report by the Governor's Juvenile Justice Commission recommended raising the age of criminal responsibility to 18. In calling for the change, the commission states:

> The commission places great weight on recent evolving brain development research that supports the position that for most 17-year-olds the necessary decision-making and moderating functions of the brain are still developing. This leads to two conclusions: (1) that although 17-year-olds are capable of "telling right from wrong" and capable of committing serious [and] violent crimes, it is not necessarily appropriate to consider them "adult-like" for purposes of prosecuting and sentencing and (2) that 17-year-olds remain more amenable to effective interventions and behavior change approaches than adults.[22]

## Struggling to Think Rationally

One of the first studies to show that the teenage brain is still in a phase of growth was released in 1999 by scientists at the University of California at Los Angeles. The study compared magnetic resonance imaging (MRI) scans of the brains in young adults between the ages of 23 and 30 with those of teenagers between the ages of 12 and 16. The images found that the amount of a fatty cell coating known as myelin, or "white matter," is slow in developing in the area of the brain known as the frontal lobe. According to the study, myelin is found in greater quantities in the brains of adults than in the brains of teenagers.

Myelin is similar to the insulation found on electrical wires. In circuits that are properly insulated, electrical current flows freely through the wires. In circuits that are improperly insulated the wires overheat, impeding the electrical current from reaching the TV set, stereo, or refrigerator. Therefore, since the brain cells in teenagers lack myelin, their frontal lobes do not do good jobs of transmitting signals to the other parts of their brains.

The frontal lobe is the place in the brain that controls behavior. "It's the part of the brain that says: 'Is this a good idea? What is the consequence of this action?'" says Frances Jensen, a neurologist at Children's Hospital in Boston, Massachusetts. "It's not that [teenagers] don't have a frontal lobe. And they can use it. But they are going to access it more slowly."[23]

## Brains Under Stress

Since they may not be using their frontal lobes to make decisions, many teenagers rely on a different part of their brains to guide them through stressful situations. Studies have shown that during periods of stress the amygdala in teenagers are much more active than the amygdala in adults. The amygdala are two almond-shaped clusters of cells found deep inside the brain. They serve as the brain's emotional center, controlling fear and recklessness, among other reactions. When adults are confronted with stressful situations, their frontal lobes take over, providing them with rational guidance through their crises. But when teens are confronted with stress, their amygdala take over, providing them with emotional responses.

The implications of this research are clear: Because their frontal lobes are not fully developed, many teenagers may struggle to think rationally during periods of stress, letting their emotions guide their conduct. Some teenagers may respond to this stress by being surly or rude to their parents or teachers while some may respond with a measure of rebelliousness—such as driving without a seatbelt, smoking cigarettes, or getting tattooed. Sometimes, these little acts of rebelliousness can grow into something more serious, such as shoplifting or other violations of the law. "I think all people do stupid things sometimes," says Rachael Fisher, an 18-year-old high school senior from Lakewood, Colorado. "It just seems like teenagers do it more often."[24]

## Prompted by Their Friends

These acts of rebelliousness or aggression may be further prompted by peer pressure. In 2011 researchers at Temple University in Philadelphia, Pennsylvania, wanted to see how the brains of teenagers react to pressure from their peers. MRI scans were conducted on teenagers and adults while they played video games that required them to drive virtual cars. The study showed that when the teenage players were told their friends were watching them play, they took more chances—such as speeding, driving recklessly through traffic, and ignoring traffic signals—than when they were told no one would be watching them play. And when they made heart-stopping turns or narrowly missed crashing into other vehicles, the MRI scans showed the regions of their brains associated with reward were much more active when they thought their friends were watching.

On the other hand, the adult players were generally not affected when told their friends would observe their game play—they took no more chances, and their brains showed no more activity, whether they played alone or in front of others. The results clearly showed that teenagers like to show off in front of people their own age—and their brains respond by giving them feelings of reward. "We think we've uncovered one very plausible explanation for why adolescents do a lot of stupid things with their friends that they wouldn't do when they are by themselves," says psychology professor Laurence Steinberg. "We've shown that just the knowledge that your friends are watching you can increase risky behavior."[25]

> "The commission places great weight on recent evolving brain development research that supports the position that for most 17-year-olds the necessary decision-making and moderating functions of the brain are still developing."[22]
>
> — Wisconsin Juvenile Justice Commission.

Moreover, as teenagers struggle with making good decisions, their brains may be under further stress if they use drugs or alcohol. According to Jensen, many studies have shown that alcohol and drugs have longer-lasting effects on teenagers than they do on adults. In other words, the adult metabolism does a better job than the teenage metabolism of ridding itself of alcohol, marijuana, and other drugs. Since alcohol and drugs have both been found to impair judgment, she says, the use of such substances by young people may be another reason they make poor decisions. "We make the point that what you did on the weekend is still with you during that test on Thursday,"[26] says Jensen.

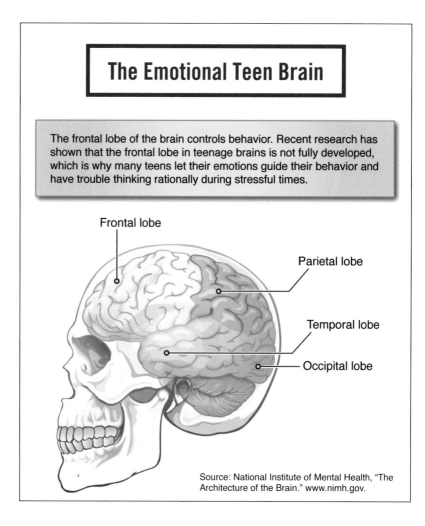

## The Emotional Teen Brain

The frontal lobe of the brain controls behavior. Recent research has shown that the frontal lobe in teenage brains is not fully developed, which is why many teens let their emotions guide their behavior and have trouble thinking rationally during stressful times.

Frontal lobe

Parietal lobe

Temporal lobe

Occipital lobe

Source: National Institute of Mental Health, "The Architecture of the Brain." www.nimh.gov.

## A Need for Positive Role Models

Despite the abundant evidence that teenagers may not realize the consequences of the bad decisions they make, many scientists, as well as legal experts, continue to insist that young people should be held responsible when their poor decisions result in criminal activity. Robert Epstein, a Harvard University–trained psychologist and former editor of *Psychology Today*, argues that the MRI scans and other evidence merely show how the brain changes but provide little evidence proving that the changes actually affect behavior. Moreover, Epstein says, while it may be true that teenagers are influenced by their peers, he suggests that young people would take fewer risks if they spent more time in the company of positive role models. He says,

Today, with teens trapped in the frivolous world of peer culture, they learn virtually everything they know from one another rather than from the people they are about to become. Isolated from adults and wrongly treated like children, it is no wonder that some teens behave, by adult standards, recklessly or irresponsibly. Almost without exception, the reckless and irresponsible behavior we see is the teen's way of declaring his or her adulthood or, through pregnancy or the commission of serious crime, of instantly becoming an adult under the law.[27]

Meanwhile, many experts contend that the vast majority of teenagers are able to deal with the emotional stresses in their lives without resorting to criminal behavior. "The overwhelming majority of teens don't join gangs and pick up guns and go out and shoot people," insists David Alkire, a former prosecutor in Monterey County, California. "The fact that a tiny minority do it is no reason to give them some benefit of the doubt that if they had better judgment and were acting as adults, they wouldn't have done this."[28]

> *"The overwhelming majority of teens don't join gangs and pick up guns and go out and shoot people."* [28]
>
> — David Alkire, former Monterey County, California, prosecutor.

Alkire, as well as other law enforcement officials and policy makers, are not prepared to give up the option of trying young people in adult courtrooms. "I think it's too soon to simply rely on that sort of [science]," says Todd Heisey, the chief deputy district attorney of Bernalillo County, New Mexico. "Some kids are just violent."[29]

## In the Hands of the Judge

Still, as many law enforcement officers, prosecutors, legislators, and other policy makers demand that juvenile offenders be tried in adult courts, more states are expected to re-examine their laws setting the minimum age of criminal responsibility. Even as those states raise their ages of criminal responsibility, they are still likely to provide the means by which young offenders can be brought to trial in adult courtrooms. In Connecticut the new law continues to provide exceptions under which young people charged with violent offenses can still be brought to trial in adult court.

## Many Teenagers Lack Empathy

People who commit violence against other people usually lack empathy toward their victims: When they hurt others, they feel no sorrow over what they have done. A study conducted by the Institute of Cognitive Neuroscience at University College in London, England, reported that in teenagers, often very little activity occurs in the medial prefrontal cortex, the portion of the brain responsible for empathetic responses.

Researchers asked adults and teenagers how they would react to a series of situations and conducted brain scans while the subjects gave their answers. In situations that called for empathetic reactions, the scans showed considerable activity in the medial prefrontal cortex of adults. In teenagers, the medial prefrontal cortex showed little activity—evidence that many teenagers find it hard to feel empathy. Says Sarah-Jayne Blakemore, a professor of neuroscience at the institute, "We think that a teenager's judgment of what they would do in a given situation is driven by the simple question: 'What would I do?' Adults, on the other hand, ask: 'What would I do, given how I would feel and given how the people around me would feel as a result of my actions?'"

Quoted in Sara Goudarzi, "Study: Teenage Brain Lacks Empathy," MSNBC, September 8, 2006. www.msnbc.msn.com.

Others believe that the best way to decide whether a case belongs in adult court is to leave the decision in the hands of the judge. In the case of Gumbs, Brenner listened to testimony from police and other witnesses, but he also listened closely to what the mental health experts had to say. And the experts told the judge that when Gumbs stood on the highway overpass and dangled a block of ice over the traffic below, he was acting as a typical teenager—a young person who may not always be thinking things through. Finally, the judge determined that the 15-year-old defendant standing in front of him may have acted impulsively and foolishly, but his act that caused Cowell's death did not equate to murder.

## Facts

- A 2007 study by Emory University in Atlanta, Georgia, indicated that most criminals commit their first violent acts between the ages of 16 and 19. After the age of 19, few people commit their first acts of violence, the study said.

- Many states cite financial reasons for raising the age of criminal responsibility. In North Carolina, a 2011 study suggested that raising the age from 16 to 18 would result in a net savings to taxpayers of $52 million, mostly realized by moving young inmates out of prisons.

- The minimum age of criminal responsibility in England, Ireland, and Wales is 10. In Scotland the age is 8, but in 2011 lawmakers approved raising it to 12. The age in Germany, Italy, and Spain is 14. France has no age of criminal responsibility.

- A 2008 report by Harvard University Medical School found that, overall, the human brain is just 80 percent developed in teenagers. Moreover, the portion of the brain controlling the power to make decisions may not be fully developed until age 30.

- A 2011 study by Dartmouth College on raising the minimum age of criminal responsibility in New Hampshire found that approximately 300 17-year-olds a year are tried in adult courts in that state, and most are charged with underage drinking or drug possession.

# CHAPTER THREE

# Do Adult Court Sentences Deter Juvenile Crime?

When Kenneth Sukhia served as a prosecutor in Florida, he brought a case against five defendants arrested for a carjacking in which a 72-year-old man had been shot and a 19-year-old college student abducted. The defendants ranged in age from 14 to 19, and all had extensive arrest records as juvenile offenders, including cases that involved violent acts. All of the defendants had been through the juvenile justice system numerous times, and yet none had served more than a few months in detention. After their releases, all had returned to committing criminal acts.

As Sukhia prepared cases against the defendants in adult court, they remained defiant. "[One defendant] told me that he had never served a day in jail and that 'you can't touch me,'"[30] Sukhia recalls. In this case, though, that defendant was wrong. Sukhia won convictions against all five. The 19-year-old defendant who fired the shot was sentenced to 20 years in prison; the other defendants also received lengthy incarcerations in prisons rather than in juvenile detention facilities.

The experience convinced Sukhia that adult sentences are highly appropriate for juvenile offenders. He says, "There can be no meaningful deterrent to ongoing juvenile crime as long as juvenile offenders believe they will never be subjected to meaningful punishment for their crimes."[31]

Other advocates disagree. They point toward the harsh conditions in American prisons—even those designed to house young people—and find them to be hardly rehabilitative. "Waiving juveniles to criminal court is not the answer to the crime situation," insists Michael P. Brown. "At best, waivers are a short-term solution to a complex social condition that will not be simplified by transferring juveniles to the jurisdiction of the criminal court. . . . They merely serve to mollify the public's desire for retribution."[32]

## The Youngest Inmates

According to the Washington, DC–based advocacy group Campaign for Youth Justice, about 65,000 inmates are incarcerated in prisons designed specifically for young offenders. Under federal law, inmates under 18 are generally not permitted to be housed in the same facilities as adult prisoners—although the law has left room for some exceptions. Therefore, states have erected separate facilities to house most of their younger inmates.

These are not juvenile detention centers, which hold young offenders found delinquent in juvenile courts. Instead, they have been built in accordance with the US Juvenile Justice and Delinquency Prevention Act. These facilities are regarded as prisons and are intended to hold young inmates until they reach adulthood, at which time they are transferred to adult prisons to complete their sentences. In most cases, inmates are 16 or 17 when they arrive in these facilities. Some defendants stay in these prisons until they reach 18 while others are permitted to remain in the facilities until the age of 21. Laws differ from state to state on when the inmates are to be moved to adult prisons.

In some cases prison inmates have been younger than 16 or 17. In 2009 prosecutors charged 11-year-old Jordan Brown of New Galilee, Pennsylvania, with the murder of his father's girlfriend. When prosecutors announced their intention to try Brown in adult court, officials at the State Correctional Institution in Pine Grove, the state's only prison for young inmates, made plans to house him. If Brown were convicted in adult court, it would mean that the Pine

> "There can be no meaningful deterrent to ongoing juvenile crime as long as juvenile offenders believe they will never be subjected to meaningful punishment for their crimes."[31]
>
> — Kenneth Sukhia, former Florida prosecutor.

Grove prison could be housing an inmate as young as 13. "It would be a whole new experience," says Bob Behr, a supervisor at Pine Grove. "We've had a few 14-year-olds enter the system, but they're usually 15 or older by the time they get here. If he comes here, that would provide many interesting challenges."[33] However, in 2011 the judge in the case transferred Brown's trial to juvenile court.

## Structured Environment

Prison life for any inmate is unpleasant. For teenagers, it can be a devastating experience. At a time when others their age are going to school, dating, playing sports, making college plans, or learning trades, these young people must live within the tiny confines of their prison cells.

Pine Grove, located about 40 miles east of Pittsburgh, was built to hold a maximum of 786 young offenders. At the prison, an inmate's day begins at 6 o'clock in the morning with a military-style workout of pushups, jumping jacks, crunches, and other exercises. "We turn on the lights and then knock individually on each locked cell door,"[34] a corrections supervisor told a reporter for the *Pittsburgh Tribune-Review*. Minor infractions of the rules often are punished with additional calisthenics—an inmate who steps over a painted line in a corridor into a restricted area could be ordered to do 50 pushups on the spot.

Inmates may have to spend their daytime hours in classes (under Pennsylvania law, all people 16 and younger must attend school, even if they are in prison) or in prison jobs—working in the kitchen, swabbing floors, or performing other manual labor. Their lives are highly regimented, with frequent inspections. Prison officials structure their days so the inmates have no time to themselves. "When you consider that many inmates arriving here have had very little or absolutely no structure during their young lives [discipline] is very important,"[35] says Douglas Russell, a public information officer for Pine Grove.

"At best, waivers are a short-term solution to a complex social condition that will not be simplified by transferring juveniles to the jurisdiction of the criminal court. . . . They merely serve to mollify the public's desire for retribution."[32]

— Michael P. Brown, Ball State University criminal justice professor.

## Cut Off from Their Families

Meanwhile, the young inmates at Pine Grove and similar institutions must live with the reality that they will be forced to remain in prison for what could be several years or even more. If they are serving long sentences, they will probably continue serving their sentences in adult prisons. Many of the young inmates grow depressed or suffer from anxiety when they realize just how much time they face behind bars. "After a while, some of them realize, 'I'm not going home,'" says Pine Grove supervisor Don Bachota. "It might be three years after they get here. No matter when it is, when they realize they [could be serving] life in prison, they don't handle it well."[36]

According to many young inmates, the hardest part of life in Pine Grove is being cut off from their families. Chally Dang, who was convicted of manslaughter at the age of 15, was sent to Pine

*Young people who are sent to adult prisons will find harsher conditions than in juvenile facilities. Overcrowding is a big problem in many prisons but it has reached critical proportions in California's San Quentin State Prison, where the prison gym has held nearly 400 double-bunked inmates (pictured).*

Grove to begin serving a sentence of five and a half to 11 years. Dang is from Philadelphia, which is in the eastern part of the state, so his family members must endure more than a five-hour drive to visit him in the western Pennsylvania prison. For many families, having to travel such distances can be a hardship, which means that visits to their young relatives are rare. Dang keeps photographs of family members in his cell—he says it is one of the few connections he still has with them. He also knows that while he is spending time in prison, he is missing the good times he could be enjoying with his friends and family members back home. "I feel like a generation has gone by,"[37] Dang said, while flipping through the pictures in his cell.

Another young Pine Grove inmate, Jason Clark, was sentenced to three to six years in prison on an armed robbery charge. Clark, who is a father, is also from the eastern part of the state—his family lives in Chester, a small city near Philadelphia. Since his incarceration, Clark says, he has hardly gotten to know his young daughter. "I've seen her maybe twice,"[38] he says.

## Life in an Adult Prison

As difficult as life in a juveniles-only prison may be for inmates like Clark and Dang, many young inmates face far harsher environments. When the Juvenile Justice and Delinquency Prevention Act was amended in 1980 to prohibit incarceration of juveniles in adult prisons, Congress left room for some exceptions. Under the amendment, a juvenile can be sent to an adult prison if authorities obtain a court order that specifically directs the young offender be incarcerated in an adult institution. According to the Campaign for Youth Justice, some 7,500 inmates under the age of 18 are housed in adult prisons.

Typically, the young inmates who are transferred to adult prisons are regarded as too violent or disruptive even for the secure juvenile prisons where they would ordinarily be housed. In 2011 authorities in New York State released videos filmed inside a juvenile facility that showed young offenders assaulting staff members, forming gangs, and physically attacking individual residents as

"After a while, some of them realize, 'I'm not going home.'"[36]

— Pine Grove State Correctional Institution supervisor Don Bachota.

# A Matter of Perception

Research shows that young offenders do not pause to consider the consequences before they commit criminal acts. In fact, researchers have found that many young offenders commit crimes under the assumption that, if caught, they would face light sentences in juvenile court—or even no punishment at all.

A joint study by Villanova and Columbia universities questioned 37 juveniles in Georgia who had been charged with either armed robbery or murder. All were tried in adult court. The researchers found that none of the young defendants thought they would be tried as adults or face time in maximum-security prisons. Rather, all 37 thought that if they were apprehended, they would at most face sentences in juvenile detention centers or similar facilities designed for young offenders. One of the defendants told the researchers, "When they caught me, I thought my momma would just come get me and I wouldn't even have to spend the night."

Most of the defendants told the researchers that, in hindsight, if they had known the penalties would have been so harsh, they never would have committed their crimes. One defendant told the researchers, "[Being tried as an adult] showed me it's not a game anymore. Before, I thought that since I'm a juvenile I could do just about anything and just get six months if I got caught. So, I didn't care and thought I could get away with anything."

Quoted in Richard E. Redding and Elizabeth J. Fuller, "What Do Juvenile Offenders Know About Being Tried as Adults? Implications for Deterrence," *Juvenile and Family Court Journal*, Summer 2004, p. 39.

well as committing acts of vandalism such as destroying furniture. The videos showed that staff members had to use force to subdue the troublemakers. Adrian Raine, a University of Southern California psychologist, says there will always be young offenders who do not respond to rehabilitation programs and are essentially irredeemable. Says Raine, "It's naïve to think many of these very violent kids are going to stop, and [that] we don't need to be protected from them."[39]

In 2011 New York prison authorities reported that they have transferred as many as 20 juveniles a year to adult prisons. Michael Sussman, an attorney who has represented New York prison staff members, says that no matter how many troublemakers are transferred out of the juvenile prisons, others soon take their places. He says, "Given the culture of the facilities, when you remove that group, another group comes in and replaces them as leaders of the same anarchy."[40]

## Physical and Sexual Assaults

When they arrive in adult prison, the young offenders will find many of the same features and routines they knew in prisons like Pine Grove. They are housed in cells and made to live under rigorous routines that are enforced from lights on in the morning until lights out at night—with one major difference: Their cellmates are older, stronger, tougher, and usually more aggressive than the young offenders may have found in their former institutions.

T.J. Parsell was 17 years old when he robbed a photo kiosk in Dearborn, Michigan, using a toy gun. Parsell claimed the incident was a prank. Nevertheless, he was sentenced to four and a half to 15 years in prison and soon found himself serving his sentence at a Michigan prison for adults. A short time after his arrival, Parsell was physically and sexually abused by the older and stronger inmates. He recalls:

> On my first day there—the same day that my classmates were getting ready for the prom—a group of older inmates spiked my drink, lured me down to a cell and raped me. And that was just the beginning. Laughing, they bragged about their conquest and flipped a coin to see which one of them got to keep me. For the remainder of my nearly five-year sentence, I was the property of another inmate.[41]

A main reason young people find themselves victims of physical and sexual assaults in adult prisons is a lack of staffing. A 2007 report by the Campaign for Youth Justice found that, generally, more staff members are assigned to juvenile institutions than are typically found in adult prisons. With fewer corrections officers on duty to keep an eye on troublemakers, the report says, older inmates have more opportunities to prey on their younger cellmates. According to the report, the typical staffing level in an adult prison is one corrections officer for every 64 inmates; in a juvenile facility, the Campaign for Youth Justice found a typical staffing level of one officer for every 8 inmates.

*Young inmates take part in a counseling session at the Pennsylvania State Correctional Institution in Pine Grove. Daily life for the young, violent offenders who are housed there is highly regimented, with frequent inspections and a strict schedule.*

# High Levels of Depression

Physical and sexual assaults are not the only problems faced by young people in adult prisons. The Campaign for Youth Justice points out that young people housed in adult institutions lack the educational opportunities that would be available to them in juvenile facilities. The organization's 2007 report found that just 40 percent of adult prisons in America provide high school classes. "Without adequate schooling, too many youth are at risk of falling further and further behind academically even though they are legally entitled to an education,"[42] says the report.

Indeed, instead of receiving their education from accredited teachers who provide them with fundamental language and math skills, young inmates receive a far different education in adult prisons: They are exposed to older convicts who share their techniques for stealing cars, breaking into houses, selling drugs, or executing all manner of other illegal activities. Said the Campaign for Youth Justice report, "Another danger caused by housing youth within adult jails is that jails expose youth to 'role models.' By exposing juveniles to a criminal culture . . . adult institutions may socialize juveniles into becoming chronic offenders."[43]

The pressures felt by young people in adult prisons—fears of sexual and physical assault, the realization that they will be locked up for many years, the lack of educational or vocational programs, the separation from friends and family members—leads to high levels of depression among these inmates. Therefore, another danger awaits young people housed in adult facilities: suicide. The Campaign for Youth Justice cites statistics showing that young people held in adult prisons are 36 times more likely to commit suicide than young inmates held in juvenile facilities. A mother named Vicky told the Campaign for Youth Justice that her son Kirk, while serving time in an adult prison, was clearly suicidal, yet authorities in the prison failed to recognize the symptoms:

"On my first day there—the same day that my classmates were getting ready for the prom—a group of older inmates spiked my drink, lured me down to a cell and raped me."[41]

— T.J. Parsell, who entered a Michigan prison at the age of 17.

Kirk requested not to be alone because he was having anxiety. Despite his request for help and regulations requiring one-hour checks on inmates in confinement, Kirk was left alone for two-and-a-half hours. When jail staff finally checked on Kirk, my son was found dead hanging by a blanket from the smoke detector in the cell.[44]

## Emotions Drive Teen Actions

Young people in prison—regardless of whether the institution is designed for young offenders or adults—are cut off from their families and friends. They are unable to participate in high school sports or plan for college or careers in the trades. They are forced to follow restrictive routines that demand high levels of discipline. Perhaps they are physically and sexually abused. All of these factors add up to a horrific way to spend one's adolescent years. It would seem that anybody exposed to this environment would do whatever they could to stay out of prison.

And yet, despite the hardships that prison life places on the young people forced to serve time, many advocates insist that sentencing the defendants to prison does not serve as a deterrent to juvenile crime. In a 2004 study, researchers in Georgia asked 37 juvenile offenders convicted of major crimes if they were aware, prior to committing the crimes, that they would be tried in adult court. Just eight of the young offenders said they knew about the state's automatic transfer law that guaranteed they would be tried as adults. "Many thought they would get only light sentences from the juvenile court,"[45] says a Department of Justice report.

The Georgia study confirmed what legal experts have suspected for years, and what psychologists and physicians have recently supported with new medical evidence: that when it comes to making decisions about committing violent or otherwise criminal acts, most young people do not pause to consider their legal strategies in the event they are caught or whether it is prudent to commit the crimes given the likelihood they would be tried in adult courts rather than juvenile courts. Instead, their actions are driven by emotion. Says

## Plea Bargains

Plea bargaining is a common strategy employed by prosecutors and defense attorneys in courtrooms throughout America. Under plea bargaining, a defendant agrees to plead guilty if the prosecutor agrees to toss out the most serious charges. As a result of a plea negotiation between the defense and prosecuting attorneys, the defendant often receives a lighter sentence while the prosecution avoids the expense and ordeal of a criminal trial.

Many juveniles are eligible for plea bargains in adult courts because they are first-time offenders. But plea bargaining is also seen as a reason many juveniles commit new crimes after serving their sentences: The lighter sentences they receive after plea bargaining fails to deter them from committing new crimes. A Columbia University study of 707 youths charged with robbery found that the prison sentences handed out in juvenile court—where plea bargaining is rare—ranged from 11 months to 34 months in juvenile detention facilities. However, the youths whose cases were transferred to adult court received prison sentences ranging from 11 months to 31 months. Advocates for tougher sentences believe juveniles receive lighter sentences in adult courts because they are allowed to plea bargain. Says Randall Heckman, a former Kent County, Michigan, judge, "If courts would respond decisively to offenders—even on the first offense—many potential offenders will be deterred from beginning careers in criminal activity."

Quoted in Joseph P. Overton and Nick Gillespie, "Juvenile Justice Requires Juvenile Responsibility," Mackinac Center for Public Policy, March 4, 1996. www.mackinac.org.

Columbia University law professor Jeffrey Fagan, "The [transfer] laws presume that juveniles are rational beings who weigh the costs and benefits of things before doing them. Well, nothing could be further from the truth. They're kids and that's what makes them kids. . . . They [are] driven by emotional and psychological factors."[46]

# Bigger Prisons, More Inmates

With evidence mounting that sentences handed out in adult courts do not seem to have much of an effect on the juvenile crime rate, many advocates are calling for lawmakers to expand the juvenile justice system—enabling more young offenders to receive counseling, psychological services, vocational training, and other services that are often not available in prison. The Pennsylvania legislature spent $71 million to build Pine Grove. Deborah Vargas, a policy analyst for the California-based advocacy group Center on Juvenile and Criminal Justice, wonders whether the money could have been better spent on efforts to divert young offenders from the adult justice system. She says, "I think that instead of spending all that money building a new prison, they could have kept them in the juvenile justice system. When they use money for prisons, it takes away from the limited resources for other [crime-prevention] programs."[47]

And yet, many experts continue to support sentencing juvenile offenders to prison terms. "The simple fact of the matter is that juveniles who commit serious and violent crimes, particularly older youth, should in most instances face adult court sanctions," says James C. Backstrom, district attorney of Dakota County, Minnesota. "So, too, must this remedy be available for youth who have committed less serious felonies who have a long history of convictions for crime after crime for which no juvenile court disposition has been effective."[48]

At Pine Grove and similar prisons for young offenders, empty cells are rare. In fact, in 2011 the Pennsylvania Department of Corrections reported that Pine Grove was housing 45 inmates per day more than it was built to accommodate. To ease the overcrowding at Pine Grove, the state government announced plans to build a 230-bed addition onto the facility, providing the prison with the capacity to house more than 1,000 young inmates.

It would seem, then, that as the debate continues over whether young inmates should be sent to prisons or to programs established for juvenile offenders, policy makers in Pennsylvania have already decided on the course of action they intend to take. They have decided to build bigger correctional institutions as they prepare to send more young people to prison.

# Facts

- A 2011 University of Texas study found that 34 percent of youthful offenders tried in Texas adult courts had already been through the juvenile system at least four times prior to their adult trials.

- According to the advocacy group Campaign for Youth Justice, by 2009 the state with the most juveniles serving sentences in adult prisons was Florida, with 393. Other top states included Connecticut, 332; North Carolina, 215; New York, 190; Arizona, 157, and Texas, 156.

- A third of all young people who are arrested will spend at least one day in an adult prison, according to the 2009 report by the Campaign for Youth Justice. Of those young offenders, 20 percent will spend six months or more locked up in adult prisons.

- Although transfer laws are designed to get tough on juvenile offenders, a 2008 US Department of Justice study found that most juvenile inmates are released from adult prisons while they are still relatively young: 80 percent are released before their twenty-first birthday, and 95 percent are released before their twenty-fifth birthday.

- The US Department of Justice reported in 2010 that among the young people committed to adult prisons each year, about 61 percent were convicted of violent acts; 23 percent of theft and other "property offenses"; 9 percent of drug charges; and the remainder of various other crimes.

# CHAPTER FOUR

# Should Juvenile Offenders Face the Death Penalty?

Scott Allen Hain, 17, and Robert Wayne Lambert, 21, were drifting across the Midwest, stealing, vandalizing, and committing other, more serious crimes as they wandered from town to town. In Kansas they had sexually assaulted two women. Arriving in Tulsa, Oklahoma, they assaulted a couple they encountered, beating the man with a claw hammer and sexually assaulting and beating the woman.

On October 6, 1987, Hain and Lambert approached a couple, Michael Haughton, 27, and Laura Lee Sanders, 22, who were sitting together in a car in a Tulsa parking lot. The two drifters flashed a knife and forced their way into the car. Hain shoved his way into the driver's seat and drove the car into the countryside. They robbed Haughton at gunpoint, then locked the couple in the trunk. After finding a remote road, Hain and Lambert parked the car and set it on fire. Hain and Lambert stood nearby, watching the car burn and listening to the cries of the two victims as they were engulfed in the blaze.

Hain and Lambert were convicted of the murders of Haughton and Sanders and received the death sentence. Jennifer Miller, Oklahoma assistant attorney general, said the jury members were well aware that Hain was a juvenile at the time he participated in the murders, and yet they could find little sympathy for him because of his age. "When a person looks at his age and the facts of this case, I just don't think it would make a difference," Miller says. "They knew he was 17, and they saw how heinous the crime was."[49]

On April 3, 2003, his appeals exhausted, Hain was strapped to a gurney in the death house of an Oklahoma prison. He was now 32 years old. An intravenous tube was inserted into Hain's arm and deadly chemicals were injected into his body.

Hain's case marks a milestone in the history of juvenile justice in America: He was the last defendant in America executed for a crime committed before reaching the age of 18.

## Long History of Executing Young People

Two years after Hain paid the ultimate price for his crime, the US Supreme Court ruled that execution of defendants for crimes committed as juveniles violates the constitutional ban on cruel and unusual punishment. By the time the court ruled on the issue, 30 states had already enacted their own laws banning capital punishment in cases of crimes committed by juveniles. Still, at the time of the ruling, 72 inmates who committed murders as juveniles were awaiting execution in the states that still permitted imposition of the death penalty on juvenile offenders. Their sentences were immediately commuted to life in prison without parole.

Prior to Hain's execution, 364 defendants who were under the age of 18 when they committed their crimes had been executed in America. In fact, America has a history of executing young people dating back to the colonial era. The first juvenile to be executed on American soil was Thomas Graunger, a 16- or 17-year-old resident of the Plymouth Colony in Massachusetts, who was tried, found guilty, and executed in 1642 for the crime of bestiality.

Over the years, many of the condemned prisoners were like Hain—they had committed their crimes as juveniles but were well into adulthood by the time their appeals were exhausted and their

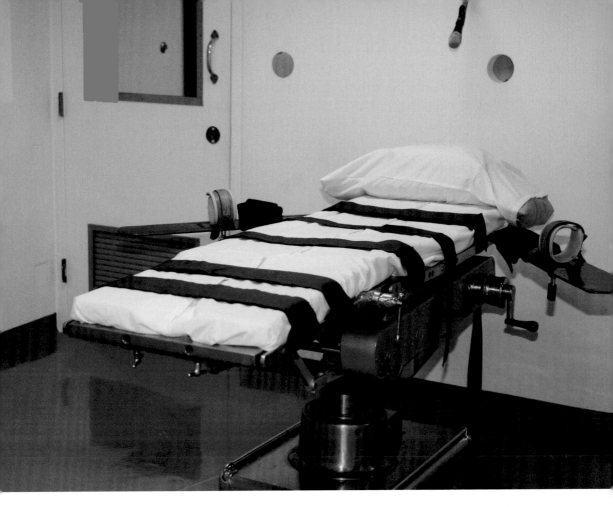

date with their executioners had arrived. Nevertheless, well into the nineteenth century, some of the condemned inmates were still children when they were put to death for their crimes. Says capital punishment historian John Laurence, "In the early part of the 19th century . . . age mattered little where the death penalty was concerned, and the legal [child], who was held to be utterly incapable of knowing what he was doing when he signed his name to a receipt, or gave an order for goods, was considered perfectly equal to understanding the heinousness of every offense against the law of the land."[50]

*Scott Allen Hain, executed in Oklahoma in 2003, was the last defendant in the United States put to death for a crime committed before age 18. Pictured is the execution chamber of the Oklahoma State Penitentiary.*

## Hanged for Their Crimes

No case illustrates this situation better than that of James Guild, who was 12 years old in 1828 when he was charged with the murder of an elderly neighbor. An indentured servant living in New Jersey, Guild had been sent to the home of Catharine Beakes to borrow a gun, but the woman refused to give it to him. Instead, she accused Guild of killing her chickens. Beakes's charges enraged Guild, and he responded by striking her with a wooden ox yoke he found hanging by the door, hitting her three times with the heavy object.

Guild later said that he struck the woman because he was afraid she would complain about him to his master, and he feared a beating. During his trial Guild was portrayed by witnesses as intelligent, but with a mean streak. One witness said, "He has as much sagacity as any boy I know of his age; was always accounted a smart, cunning mischievous boy."[51]

Guild was convicted of the murder and sentenced to death by hanging. He was hanged on November 28, 1828. As the trap door opened beneath his feet, Guild shook off his black hood and managed to balance himself on his toes at the edge of the trap-door opening. The sheriff was forced to give the boy a shove so he would fall through the opening in the gallows floor.

Throughout the remainder of the nineteenth century, until the arrival of the reform movement and establishment of separate juvenile courts, the executions of children were rare in America, but other young people did suffer the same fate as Guild. During the 1800s, 10 defendants under the age of 14 were hanged for their crimes.

## Mitigating Circumstances

During the twentieth century, as most laws governing juvenile crime were reformed to treat young offenders under different rules than had been established for adults, state laws continued to contain provisions for executing defendants who committed their crimes as juveniles. (Virtually all death penalties are handed down in cases involving homicides; a handful of states have established laws that provide for capital punishment in cases of rape against children.) Juvenile justice advocates petitioned the US Supreme Court several times to outlaw the death penalty for young defendants. Throughout most of this era, however, the nation's highest court steadfastly found that, when it comes to crimes punishable

## Where Juveniles Are Executed

By 2011 just three countries were believed to sanction the death penalty for citizens under the age of 18—Iran, Saudi Arabia, and Sudan. According to the advocacy group Human Rights Watch, in 2009 Iran executed five juvenile offenders, Saudi Arabia executed two young defendants, and Sudan executed one. In 2010 Iran is believed to have executed one juvenile offender.

Prior to the abolition of the death penalty for juvenile offenders in America, more than a century had passed since the last person under the age of 18 was put to death. Typically, all defendants were adults when the executions took place because of the lengthy appeals processes that exists in the American court system.

That is often not true in places like Iran, Saudi Arabia, and Sudan. Appeals are limited in those countries. In many cases, the death penalty is carried out within months of the commission of the crime. The human rights group Amnesty International reported that in 2007, Iran executed 24 defendants whose crimes were committed before they reached the age of 18. In 11 of those cases, the defendants were still under 18 when their sentences were carried out.

by the death penalty, juveniles should be treated under similar rules as adults.

This attitude started changing in 1982 when the court ruled in a case involving 16-year-old Monty Lee Eddings. In 1977 Eddings and some friends jumped into a car and sped off on an aimless, two-state joy ride that ended in Oklahoma where they were pulled over by state trooper Larry Crabtree. As Crabtree approached the car, Eddings fired a shotgun, killing the officer. Eddings was tried as an adult, convicted, and sentenced to death.

Five years later Eddings's appeal reached the Supreme Court. Although the court upheld the death penalty for juvenile offenders, the justices elected to commute the sentence for Eddings to life in prison. The court found that the jury in the Eddings case should have been instructed by the trial judge to consider the youth of the defendant as a mitigating factor when it convened to consider a sentence for the teenager.

Under law, all juries in death penalty cases are asked to consider elements of the case that fall into mitigating and aggravating circumstances. Mitigating circumstances are those that would lead juries to consider leniency—such as a mental illness suffered by the defendant that may have thrust him or her into a burst of violence. Aggravating circumstances are those that would lead juries to lean toward the death penalty; in many death penalty cases, the torture of the victim is regarded as an aggravating factor.

Under the Supreme Court's decision in the Eddings case, youth could now be considered a mitigating factor and, the court ruled, trial judges have the responsibility to advise juries that the youth of the defendant could be a reason to consider leniency. "Youth is more than a chronological fact," Supreme Court Justice Lewis Powell wrote in 1982. "It is a time of life when a person may be the most susceptible to influence and psychological damage. Our history is replete with laws and judicial recognition that minors, especially in their earlier years, are generally less mature and responsible than adults."[52]

## Public Standards of Decency

The Eddings case established that jurors should regard youth as a mitigating factor when considering the death penalty—but the Supreme Court's ruling still left intact state laws that permitted the executions of young people. Six years after the Eddings decision, though, the Supreme Court struck down the death penalty in all cases in which the defendants are 15 years old or younger during the commission of their crimes.

That case, which was heard by the Supreme Court in 1988, involved a 15-year-old defendant in another Oklahoma murder. William Wayne Thompson participated in the murder of his brother-in-law, shooting, stabbing, and drowning Charles Keene because Keene had allegedly been abusing Thompson's sister. The court found that the death penalty against Thompson and other defendants his age violated the constitutional guarantee against cruel and unusual punishment.

Writing for the court, Justice John Paul Stevens points out that the American public's "evolving standard of decency"[53] no longer considers the execution of a 15-year-old defendant as acceptable, whereas a century ago the death penalty against someone that young would not have been considered cruel and unusual. Justice Sandra Day O'Connor adds, "Evolving standards of decency . . . mark the progress of a maturing society."[54]

## "Relic of the Past"

Following the Eddings and Thompson decisions, death penalty opponents believed the Supreme Court was very close to outlawing executions for defendants who were 16 or 17 when they committed their crimes. The case they hoped would finally end executions of juveniles arrived at the Supreme Court a year after the Thompson case. This case involved 17-year-old Kevin Stanford, a heavy drug user who had a long record of committing crimes, including burglary, arson, and assault. In January 1981 Stanford and two others robbed a Kentucky gas station where they found a lone attendant on duty, 20-year-old Baerbel Poore, who worked at the station to support her infant daughter. Stanford and another defendant raped Poore in the gas station lavatory, then drove her to a secluded area where Stanford shot the woman twice in the head. Their take from the robbery: $143 in cash and 300 cartons of cigarettes.

Stanford was tried as an adult and sentenced to death. In his case, the court upheld the sentence. Writing the majority opinion in 1989, Justice Antonin Scalia found that, at the time, just a handful of states banned capital punishment for 16- and 17-year-olds—evidence that society still regards murder committed by young offenders to be outside the boundaries of what is decent. Writes Scalia, "In determining whether a punishment violates evolving standards of decency, this court looks not to its own subjective conceptions, but, rather, to the conceptions of modern American society as reflected by objective evidence."[55] In the Stanford case, the court found the crime was both horrific and well

"*Evolving standards of decency . . . mark the progress of a maturing society.*"[54]

— Justice Sandra Day O'Connor.

outside the boundaries of decency; the sentence was, therefore, neither cruel nor unusual.

Not all the justices agreed. Stanford's sentence was upheld by a 5-4 majority, meaning four justices cast votes against imposition of the death penalty on 16- and 17-year-old defendants. Writing for the minority, Stevens says, "Offenses committed by juveniles under the age of 18 do not merit the death penalty. The practice of executing such offenders is a relic of the past and is inconsistent with evolving standards of decency in a civilized society. We should put an end to this shameful practice."[56]

Stanford would ultimately escape execution. On his last day in office in 2003, Kentucky governor Paul E. Patton—who said he opposed the executions of juvenile defendants—exercised his power to commute Stanford's sentence to life in prison. "As a country, we need to exempt youthful offenders from capital punishment," says Cornell University professor of human development Joan Jacobs Brumberg. "Kentucky's governor understood this and set matters right."[57]

> "In determining whether a punishment violates evolving standards of decency, this court looks not to its own subjective conceptions, but, rather, to the conceptions of modern American society as reflected by objective evidence."[55]
>
> — Justice Antonin Scalia.

## Majority of States Outlaw Executing Juveniles

Between the Supreme Court's decision in the Stanford case and the execution of Hain, 18 offenders were executed in the United States for crimes they committed as juveniles. Seventeen of the defendants were 17 years old when they committed murder; one defendant was 16. All were at least 24 years old when their appeals ran out and they were executed. One defendant, Joseph Cannon, managed to extend his appeals until he reached the age of 38—21 years after he was charged with the murder of a 45-year-old woman. But on April 22, 1998, Cannon was strapped to a gurney in the death house of a Texas prison, and the sentence of the court was carried out.

The case that would finally decide the issue involved 17-year-old defendant Christopher Simmons, who in 1993 robbed and kidnapped a neighbor, Shirley Crook, tied her up, and threw her off a railroad bridge into the Meramec River in Missouri, where

# Ending Life Without Parole

Although the US Supreme Court has thrown out life-without-parole terms for juveniles for crimes other than murder, juvenile justice advocates believe the court should go a step further and give young people convicted of murder opportunities for release. According to the American Academy of Child Adolescent Psychiatry (AACAP), more than 2,500 people are serving sentences of life without parole for murders they committed while they were juveniles. AACAP has called for abolishment of all life-without-parole sentences for young offenders.

The American Civil Liberties Union (ACLU) is also advocating for an end to life-without-parole sentences for juveniles in homicide cases. In 2011 the ACLU represented defendants in two Michigan cases that the organization hoped would lead to an abolishment of life-without-parole laws for juveniles. In one case, 17-year-old Jennifer Pruitt was sentenced to life without parole after participating in a robbery in which the victim was killed by someone else. In the other case, 16-year-old Kevin Boyd was sentenced to life without parole because the court found he had helped his mother kill his father. In Boyd's case, the ACLU said, he had simply given his mother the keys to his father's house.

"Sentencing children to die in prison completely disregards their capacity for rehabilitation," says Steven Watt, staff attorney with the ACLU Human Rights Program. "In America, we should be giving children an opportunity to turn their lives around—not locking them up and throwing away the key."

Quoted in Eartha Jane Melzer, "ACLU Argues Against Mandatory Life Sentences for Kids," *Michigan Messenger*, April 22, 2011. http://michiganmessenger.com.

she drowned. Simmons was convicted and sentenced to death, but his conviction was overturned by the Missouri Supreme Court which found that it did not pass the evolving standards of decency test that had been at the core of the Thompson case. Prosecutors appealed, and in 2005 the US Supreme Court ruled on the case.

This time, the court ruled in a 5-4 majority that executions are unconstitutional for any defendants who were under the age of 18 when they committed the crime. By now, several more states had acted on their own to abolish the death penalty for juveniles. The court found that a majority of states now outlawed the death penalty for juveniles, providing evidence to the justices that the public's standards of decency had evolved toward the position that most Americans found the execution of juveniles abhorrent.

Moreover, the justices noted that other evidence had been accumulating in the meantime—most notably the scientific proof that teenagers may not comprehend the full consequences of their actions. Writing for the court, Justice Anthony M. Kennedy says he believes that juveniles are unlike adults because even those convicted of murder are capable of rehabilitation. "From a moral standpoint, it would be misguided to equate the failings of a minor with those of an adult, for a greater possibility exists that a minor's character deficiencies will be reformed,"[58] he says.

> "As a country, we need to exempt youthful offenders from capital punishment."[57]
>
> — Cornell University professor of human development Joan Jacobs Brumberg.

## Unfair to the Victims

Kennedy says he was also troubled by the fact that in the previous few years, many countries that had permitted executions of juveniles—including nations headed by dictatorial regimes in Yemen and China—rescinded their laws permitting the death penalty for young offenders. Moreover, Kennedy found that international human rights groups are pressuring other countries to cease the executions of juveniles. Writes Kennedy, "It is proper that we acknowledge the overwhelming weight of international opinion against the juvenile death penalty, resting in large part on the understanding that the instability and emotional imbalance of young people may often be a factor in the crime."[59]

The ruling was criticized by many people who support capital punishment. Dianne Clements, president of Justice

**Rumbaugh** **Cannon** **Harris** **Pinkerton**

**Carter** **Garrett** **Cantu** **Mitchell**

*The eight Texas death row inmates pictured here were under age 18 when they committed their crimes. All were executed, including Joseph Cannon (top, second from left), whose appeals finally ran out at the age of 38.*

for All, a Houston, Texas–based group that advocates for the rights of victims, said the ruling is unfair to the families of victims slain by juveniles. "The Supreme Court has opened the door for more innocent people to suffer by 16- and 17-year-olds,"[60] she says. Meanwhile, some advocates insisted that the death penalty serves as a deterrent to violent crime committed by youths. Says Don Boys, a former Indiana state legislator,

> The message to kids should be clear, concise, and conclusive. No free ride until 18. No anonymity. No blaming poverty, parents, or potty training for criminality. No more community service for rape and murder. Even the dullest teen will understand that society considers leniency lunacy and a thing of the past.

> Kids think they can get away with murder and they will continue to believe that until citizens force the criminal justice system to get its act together. When a few teens "walk the last mile" other teens will get the message that sane, sensible, and scared people are taking over from the bleating [bleeding] hearts.[61]

The Supreme Court's ruling was welcomed by advocates who had long questioned the appropriateness of death penalties for young offenders. Says James Alan Fox, professor of criminal justice at Northeastern University in Boston, Massachusetts:

> Teenagers may look like, act like and even shoot like adults, but they think like children. . . . The death penalty's deterrent effect, if any, surely vanishes for adolescents, who tend not to consider consequences. Immediate rewards and punishments—peers' praise or rejection, for example—are far more critical than what the justice system might one day do to them.
>
> Teens are risk-takers. Much of their reckless behavior—poor driving, drug use, unprotected sex—carries a potential "death sentence," yet they play the odds. It is unreasonable to expect that capital punishment will make them think twice, when so often they don't even think once.[62]

## Abolishing Life Without Parole

Five years after the Supreme Court's 2005 ruling on capital punishment and young offenders, the court rendered another ruling that greatly affected juvenile justice. The court ruled that sentencing juvenile offenders to life in prison without parole for any offense other than murder is also in violation of the constitutional provision against cruel and unusual punishment.

The Supreme Court ruled on an appeal brought by attorneys for Terrance Graham who, at the age of 16, robbed a restaurant in Jacksonville, Florida. He was sentenced to a year in prison and three years' probation. Shortly after his release, Graham, now just 17 years old, broke into a private home and committed a robbery. The judge decided that Graham was incorrigible and sentenced the young defendant to life in prison.

Kennedy again wrote the opinion for the court, finding that there are two categories of crimes: those in which the lives of innocent people are taken, and those in which there is no loss of life. In cases in which lives are not lost, Kennedy said, states violate the constitutional provision against cruel and unusual punishment if they do not provide juvenile offenders with realistic opportunities to win parole.

In his opinion, Kennedy cites evidence showing that just 129 juvenile offenders were currently incarcerated for life for crimes not involving murder. That statistic, he says, indicates that states rarely impose the penalty and, therefore, there is no public demand for life terms for juveniles whose crimes fall short of murder. Despite the rarity of the sentence, at the time of the court's ruling 37 states, as well as the federal government, had adopted statutes imposing life sentences on juveniles for crimes other than murder. All of those statutes were tossed out as a result of the court's ruling.

The court voted 6-3 in 2010 to abolish life-without-parole penalties on juveniles in cases that don't involve murder. Writing a dissenting opinion, Justice Clarence Thomas says he believes some crimes are so heinous that they should still merit life sentences even if no lives are taken. Writes Thomas, "The court is quite willing to accept that a 17-year-old who pulls the trigger on a firearm can demonstrate sufficient depravity and irredeemability to be denied re-entry into society, but insists that a 17-year-old who rapes an 8-year-old and leaves her for dead does not."[63]

*"The Supreme Court has opened the door for more innocent people to suffer by 16- and 17-year-olds."*[60]

— Dianne Clements, president of Justice for All.

## Protected Against the Ultimate Punishment

The Supreme Court's decisions in the Simmons and Graham cases illustrate that after the get-tough attitude toward juvenile offenders in the 1980s and 1990s, society has once again adopted the notion that the law should treat young people who commit crimes differently than it treats adults. As Laurence pointed out, during the nineteenth century juveniles were not to be trusted to do the family's grocery shopping by themselves, but they were considered old enough to know how they would be treated by the law should they commit violence against another person.

It took more than a century, but the nation's highest court finally decided that while young offenders may still be committing acts of violence against other people, they are not old enough to truly understand the consequences of their conduct. As the court ruled in the Thompson and Simmons cases, society's evolving standards of decency have had a lot to do with this new attitude toward the treatment of juveniles who kill. And so the court has ruled that when young people commit murder, they should be protected against society's ultimate punishment.

## Facts

- The youngest boy executed in America was James Arcene, who was 10 when he was hanged for an Arkansas murder and robbery in 1885; the youngest girl was Hannah Ocuish, 12, executed in Connecticut in 1786 for the murder of a 6-year-old playmate.

- When the US Supreme Court abolished life-without-parole sentences for juveniles who commit crimes other than murder, Florida was the state with the most inmates serving those sentences. The Florida total was 77. Second on the list was Louisiana with 17.

- When the US Supreme Court outlawed the death penalty for juveniles, the state with the most juvenile offenders on death row was Texas with 29. Alabama placed second with 14. No other state had more than five.

- One of the youngest defendants to have been executed for a crime other than murder is Fortune Ferguson, who was 13 years old when he was executed in Florida in 1927 after his conviction on a rape charge.

- According to the National Conference of State Legislatures, by 2010 Pennsylvania was the state with the most inmates serving life-without-parole terms for crimes they committed as juveniles, with 475 inmates incarcerated. Other top states included Michigan with 346, Louisiana with 335, and California with 250.

# Can Juvenile Offenders Be Rehabilitated?

Elmer Blanco had been bullied by a classmate for months. Unable to stand further abuse, the New York City high school student challenged the bully to a fight—which Blanco won when he smashed a soda bottle across the face of his opponent. The blow opened a deep cut in the bully's face, requiring several stitches.

Blanco, 15, was arrested and sent to juvenile court. He was found delinquent and ordered to serve a nine-month sentence at a juvenile detention facility in upstate New York. When he arrived, Blanco found that the center was not the prison he expected. Instead, it was modeled after boot camps young recruits are sent to when they enter the military—complete with military-style fatigues to wear and former drill sergeants as staff.

Rising before dawn each morning, Blanco and the other detainees found themselves facing rigorous days of exercise, academic classes, and counseling sessions that included anger management and help with avoiding substance abuse. "It was hell at first, physically and emotionally," says Blanco. "You had to do everything when they told you to. In the first few weeks, I spent a lot of time standing. We did push-ups, sit-ups, doing the obstacle course, rappelling."[64]

After completing his sentence, Blanco returned to high school, graduated, and enrolled in a community college. He is convinced that the personal discipline he learned at boot camp changed his life and has helped keep him out of trouble. He says, "Now if somebody picks on me, I still might be angry but I'll let it go."[65]

*Inmates at a state-run juvenile boot camp in Alabama line up for outdoor physical training activities. Schooling, counseling, and rigorous exercise and discipline form the core of boot camp programs for juvenile offenders.*

## Programs for Habitual Offenders

The environment found by Blanco at a boot camp for juvenile offenders illustrates the difference between the sentences handed out in the juvenile justice system and those administered by the adult criminal court system. In the adult system, the sentence is meant to be punitive, which often means the defendant is sent to prison. In the juvenile justice system, the emphasis is on rehabilitation. Certainly, as Blanco learned, the routine and discipline of a boot camp can be strenuous, but he emerged from the experience a better person, willing to pursue a law-abiding life.

Boot camps are only one option that juvenile court judges have at their disposal as they examine a young offender's background and the nature of his or her crime. After evaluating testimony at the delinquency hearing from law enforcement officers, social workers, family members, mental health experts, and other witnesses, the judge may elect to send the delinquent youth to a highly structured environment where discipline is emphasized, or to a minimum-security, community-based program where the offender will be granted a large measure of freedom. The programs vary greatly from state to state because state and local governments tailor these programs to meet their specific needs.

The most secure of these programs are maximum-security detention centers: high-security places for juvenile offenders who have been judged delinquent in felony cases. These offenders are considered escape risks or are known to be violent. Often known as serious or habitual offender programs, these facilities are similar to prisons in that they employ physical security features to ensure protection of the public, such as locked doors and razor wire fences. These centers typically hold no more than 25 male delinquents between the ages of 14 and 18, although some states permit 19-year-old offenders to remain in the programs. Residents attend academic classes on-site. They may also receive mental health, substance abuse, and behavior management counseling. Most offenders can expect to remain in a serious or habitual offender program for nine to twelve months.

Youth development centers also provide a high degree of security. As with the maximum-security detention centers, residents can expect to spend their time in these facilities behind locked doors and razor wire fences, and its programs are intended for young offenders found delinquent in felony cases. These centers are modern versions of the old reform schools, providing academic and vocational training to the residents. Mental health, substance abuse, and behavior management counseling are also provided to the residents, who typically stay up to nine months in these facilities.

## Wilderness Camps

Unlike their counterparts in maximum-security detention centers or youth development centers, residents of wilderness camps are not confined behind razor wire or locked doors—mostly because these camps, as the name suggests, are often located many miles from cities or towns. Indeed, young offenders who may be inclined to run away from the camps would quickly find themselves lost in the woods with no food and no idea how to get home.

Typically, wilderness programs maintain populations of 20 to 25 male delinquents between the ages of 15 and 18, although it is not unusual for female delinquents to attend wilderness camps. Most delinquent youths can expect to spend up to a year in a wilderness camp. The camps provide academic classes as well as mental health, substance abuse, and behavior management counseling. Mostly, though, residents of the camps learn how to work—they cut trails, build cabins, and perform other labor-intensive work outdoors. Ted Wisniewski, director of a wilderness camp in North Carolina, says the camps are effective because they take juvenile offenders out of the types of environments where they can find trouble. At the camps, he says, the young offenders learn about the value of teamwork. "Alternative residential life simplifies life for kids," he says. "They grow in character."[66]

Wisniewski directs Camp E-Tik-Etu, which is operated by the nonprofit organization Eckerd Youth Alternatives under a contract with the North Carolina Department of Juvenile Justice. One graduate of the camp is Trevor Castleman, who says the camp helped him learn how to control his anger. "The camp changed my life," he says. "My parents and I were always in conflict. We could never get along. I had no anger management skills."[67] Castleman returned to high school after spending 11 months at the wilderness camp. After he finishes high school, Castleman says, he plans to enlist in the military.

Many western states have established ranch camps in place of wilderness camps. The concept is the same as a wilderness camp, but the environment is different. As the name suggests, these camps are established on working ranches where young offenders work around horses and other livestock and learn the skills of ranch hands.

## Community-Based Programs

As with wilderness and ranch camps, boot camps are typically located in remote areas. Boot camps provide offenders with military-style discipline. During the first two weeks at a typical boot camp,

*"Alternative residential life simplifies life for kids. They grow in character."*[66]

— Ted Wisniewski, director of a North Carolina wilderness camp.

the residents are schooled in the military lifestyle and learn the rules and regulations of their facilities. Boot camps often feature a silence rule—residents are not permitted to speak to one another except under special circumstances. Their days are spent engaged in tough military-style discipline, including drilling and physical training. They are given little to no free time or recreation.

In fact, the only times the residents are not saluting, marching, rappelling, or double-timing it to their activities are during mess, after lights out, or when they are in class for their mandatory academic training. Boot camps also feature mental health and substance abuse counseling.

All of these programs are regarded as high security—the public is protected from the offenders either by locked doors and razor wire or by the remoteness of the wilderness camps or boot camps. After graduating from these facilities, the delinquents may qualify for programs that give them far more freedom and less supervision. In addition, delinquent youths whose offenses are nonviolent or

*High-security features, such as locked doors and razor wire fences, are built into some juvenile detention centers. A 16-foot-high fence surrounds this county juvenile detention center in New Mexico.*

otherwise minor may be sent directly to these minimum-security programs by the juvenile courts. These programs are based in the community, meaning that the offenders have the freedom to leave these facilities during the day to attend school or go to work.

Group homes, often called halfway houses, typically represent the first step back into the community for most young offenders. Staff members maintain supervision in the houses and also provide counseling for mental health issues, substance abuse, and behavior management. Most halfway houses serve from 15 to 30 residents between the ages of 15 and 18.

Of course, the programs that offer the least security are those that enable the delinquents to remain at home. Under a judge's order, the offenders may have to perform some measure of community service, such as cleaning ambulances or picking up litter along roads. Typically, they are supervised by juvenile probation officers who may visit them at their homes periodically during the term of their probation. Delinquents who qualify for these programs are usually first-time offenders as well as others whose offenses are regarded as minor and nonviolent.

> "They start changing your morals and getting them straight. They teach you to push yourself when things get hard, not to give up."[68]
>
> —Texas boot camp participant Ryan Armstrong.

## Few Opportunities in Prison

Regardless of whether the offenders are sent to boot camps, wilderness camps, habitual offender programs, or halfway houses, the overriding philosophy guiding the juvenile justice system is rehabilitation. The young offenders learn not only skills that help them with self-discipline, but also teamwork, self-esteem, respect for authority, and how to follow rules. "When you first get here, they strip you down of what you knew on the streets," says 15-year-old Ryan Armstrong, who was sentenced to a term at a boot camp in Hays County, Texas. "They start changing your morals and getting them straight. They teach you to push yourself when things get hard, not to give up."[68]

On the other hand, rehabilitation is only one of the aims of a penal system, whether it is designed for adult or juvenile offenders. Moreover, rehabilitation is often an aim that is neglected due to budgetary restraints or get-tough attitudes by political leaders who

## Can Teens Be Scared Straight?

Many juvenile offender programs have adopted a "scared straight" strategy by requiring delinquents to make visits to prisons as part of their rehabilitation programs. During the visits they tour the prisons to observe living conditions, and they also receive harsh lectures from inmates about the life that awaits them behind bars.

At the Maryland Correctional Institution in Jessup, Maryland, young offenders are regularly brought into the prison. "Somebody can come in here and bust your head wide open!" an inmate told 13-year-old Sahn, who had been arrested for shoplifting six times. "Do you want to be left that way? In a puddle of blood?"

The strategy was first chronicled in the documentary film *Scared Straight!* which follows a group of juvenile offenders as they spend several hours with convicted criminals at Rahway State Prison in New Jersey. At the conclusion of the documentary, the teenage offenders admit that the inmates' warnings have frightened them into leading lives on the straight and narrow—in other words, they are scared straight. The film won a 1978 Academy Award as Best Documentary.

The US Department of Justice does not support scared straight programs. The department has taken the position that positive role models have a far more rehabilitative effect on young offenders than warnings related by prisoners.

Quoted in Kristin Lewis, "Can Violent Criminals Help Troubled Teens?," *Scholastic Scope*, April 4 2011, p. 4.

oversee state and local corrections departments. The other principles that guide corrections administrators—the desire to punish the offender and protect society—often take precedence in prisons.

Shaun Miller knows all about prison life. He had been through the juvenile system after stealing a car. After participating in the robbery of a convenience store in Nevada, Miller was tried in adult court and sentenced to a term of 6 to 15 years in a state prison. He entered the Nevada prison system at the age of 15.

Nevada has established a prison for youthful offenders at the Southern Desert Correctional Center in Indian Springs, 55 miles north of Las Vegas. Miller is one of 45 inmates incarcerated at the facility. Life at the prison is dull and can be dangerous—many inmates have violent backgrounds. Also, the facility provides virtually no rehabilitative programs. Due to budgetary constraints, the state government has been unable to provide vocational training programs for the young offenders. According to Miller, life in prison seems to be one endless, boring day after another. "It's just a bunch of criminals inside a barbed-wire fence," he says. "The only thing you do is walk around and listen to everyone tell their criminal stories."[69]

Miller does not know what he will do when he is released. When he leaves prison, Miller says, he will be a ninth-grade dropout with a felony conviction on his record. "What am I going to do?" he asks. "I never had no job. I don't have no job skills."[70]

> "It's just a bunch of criminals inside a barbed-wire fence. The only thing you do is walk around and listen to everyone tell their criminal stories."[69]
>
> — Teenage prison inmate Shaun Miller.

## High Probability of Recidivism

There is, in fact, a high probability that former inmates like Miller will return to lives of crime. Although a national study assessing recidivism rates for juvenile offenders has never been done, some states have conducted their own studies, and many have concluded that juveniles sentenced in adult courts are more likely to commit additional crimes than offenders who go through juvenile systems. "Studies show that transfer fails to deter violent juvenile offenders," says Enrico Pagnanelli, a Philadelphia attorney and former editor of the *American Criminal Law Review*. "In fact, various studies have indicated that transfer actually increases recidivism among these offenders. This increased recidivism manifests a failure to deter, a failure to rehabilitate, and most significantly, a failure to protect society."[71]

A 2002 Florida study found that young people released from prisons commit 34 percent more crimes than those who are released from juvenile facilities. The Florida study followed 950 offenders after completion of their sentences—475 had served time in prison while 475 were committed to juvenile programs. "The conclusion . . . is that transfer [to adult court] increases recidivism," said the report. "Transfer is more likely to aggravate recidivism than to stem it."[72]

The Florida researchers interviewed many of the young offenders whose behaviors were chronicled in the report. According to the young people who were interviewed, the differences between the juvenile and adult systems were evident from the moment they arrived in the courtroom. One young offender describes his first contact with the juvenile court judge: "He had a talk with me in his office . . . just me and him. He said it was time for me to straighten up. . . . I never thought a judge would sit and talk to me that long, spend his working hours with me. He really cared about me. He was talking to me in a tone like a dad talks to you. It had a big impact on me."[73]

## Cold and Impersonal

On the other hand, the Florida researchers found most young defendants transferred into the adult system had far different feelings about their experiences. Most described their trips through the adult court system as cold and impersonal. Indeed, these offenders said their opportunities for rehabilitation seemed to be the matters of least concern among the judges and lawyers they encountered. One juvenile offender says,

> I had a public defender, a paid attorney working for the state. . . . He said he was going to get me out. Then a couple months down the road I got a letter from him saying that the state offered a plea bargain for three and a half years in prison with three years probation and $1,800 restitution. I didn't understand that I was going to [prison].

> *"Transfer is more likely to aggravate recidivism than to stem it."*[72]
>
> — Florida Department of Juvenile Justice.

The attorney made this deal without talking to me about it, told me it was my best shot 'cause I could get 30 years if I got found guilty. He said I'd be out in six months with [good behavior] so I took it. I don't think he did a good job for me . . . I was naïve.[74]

According to Pagnanelli, when young people leave prison—whether they serve their sentences in adult prisons or juveniles-only prisons—they reenter society as different individuals. For starters, they are stigmatized by their experiences behind bars. They find fewer opportunities available in employment because many employers do not want to hire convicted criminals. Many of these youths feel as though they have been wronged by the system—to have received such harsh treatment at such a young age—and therefore they carry combative attitudes back into society. "A juvenile who has been tried in a criminal court often feels unjustly treated," he says. "Extensive interviews with juvenile offenders in the adult criminal system reveal that they view the system as duplicitous and manipulative, malevolent in intent, and indifferent to their needs."[75] Ultimately, Pagnanelli says, this attitude leads them back to crime.

## Prisons Are Punitive and Dangerous

The Florida researchers conducted several interviews with young offenders about their experiences in prisons as well as in juvenile programs. Clearly, these interviews showed that prison life was punitive, often dangerous, and far from rehabilitative. "All of this is like one big, long day," says one former inmate. "Bars, steel, concrete—every day just like the next. There [are] limited things to do. . . . The only thing that makes it different is confrontations with different inmates on different days."[76]

As for the corrections officers on duty in the prisons, the young offenders said their main jobs were to keep order and make sure everyone followed the rules—not to oversee the rehabilitative opportunities for the inmates. "Staff will send you to [solitary confinement] for something petty rather than have you learn something," reports one inmate. "They could care less about the inmates. They are mean-spirited."[77]

# The Cost of Rehabilitating Juveniles

Advocates for rehabilitating young offenders argue that some state lawmakers favor incarcerating juveniles in prisons because it is cheaper than rehabilitating them in juvenile programs. According to an analysis by the Washington, DC–based Justice Policy Institute, state governments spend an average of $240 a day to house an offender in a boot camp, juvenile detention facility, group home, or similar program. Meanwhile, the US Department of Justice reports that it costs an average of $62 a day to house an inmate in a state prison.

Juvenile programs are more expensive because they often provide counseling, education, vocational training, and other rehabilitative services that many prisons do not provide. On the other hand, Neelum Arya, the director of research for the advocacy group Campaign for Youth Justice, argues that the long-term costs of prisons are higher than those associated with juvenile programs.

Such costs include those associated with police, who must arrest the repeat offenders, as well as the prisons which must house the inmates for longer periods of times. Also, she says, among the costs not reflected in the statistics are those incurred by the victims of the crimes committed by repeat offenders. Because former prison inmates are more likely to commit crimes again than the young people who have graduated from rehabilitation programs, "Incarcerating youth in adult prison is the most expensive option that consistently produces the worst results," she says.

Quoted in Martha T. Moore, "States Change Laws, Send Fewer Juveniles to Adult Court," *USA Today*, March 16, 2011. www.usatoday.com.

When the Florida researchers interviewed offenders who had spent time in juvenile programs, they found a far different attitude. One former resident of a secure residential program told the researchers, "They put you in a lot of groups, [with] feedback . . . then they let you play sports and stuff; it was a good program. . . . It made me change a lot, gave [me] some respect for people and myself. . . . They taught me most about anger control, bein' respectful of peers and myself."[78]

## Contradictory Statistics

However, not all studies have found higher recidivism rates among juveniles who have been through adult courts. A 2011 study of the North Carolina juvenile justice system found just a slight difference in recidivism rates, reporting that 25 percent of juveniles convicted in adult court committed new crimes while the recidivism rate for those tried in juvenile court is 23 percent—nearly a statistical tie between the two systems of justice.

Moreover, the study found that as the young offenders grew older, their recidivism rates decreased. The study found, for example, that the recidivism rate for 12-year-old offenders was 51 percent while for 15-year-old offenders, the recidivism rate dropped to 37 percent. The reason? The authors of the study speculated that as juvenile offenders grow older their opportunities to commit more crimes decline because many of them are in prison.

Given the contradictory statistics offered by such research projects as the North Carolina and Florida recidivism studies, some experts contend that recidivism statistics should not be regarded as a significant factor in judging the success of juvenile rehabilitation programs. A 2006 US Department of Justice report said recidivism statistics are wholly based on the arrest records of the offenders. The report said that many former inmates are likely to be repeat offenders who manage to escape arrest. Therefore, recidivism studies are highly flawed because they do not include repeat offenders who get away with their crimes. Says the Justice Depart-

"Virtually all measures of recidivism underestimate re-offenders since they only include offending that comes to the attention of the system."[79]

— North Carolina Sentencing and Policy Advisory Commission.

ment study, "Virtually all measures of recidivism underestimate re-offenders since they only include offending that comes to the attention of the system."[79]

## Programs of Intervention

Regardless of the accuracy of the recidivism statistics, juvenile rehabilitation programs clearly do not always work—many young people leave the programs and soon commit new crimes. Experts agree that a much more effective method of helping young people stay out of trouble is to intervene in their lives before they turn to crime. The Office of Juvenile Justice and Delinquency Prevention in the US Department of Justice has recommended that political leaders, judges, and other policy makers endorse programs that provide interventions in the lives of troubled youths. According

*A Michigan program pairs troubled youth with abandoned dogs awaiting adoption. Participants are responsible for the care, grooming, and training of the dogs. Community-based programs such as this one encourage young people to become more responsible and compassionate.*

to the agency, these programs should engage schools, religious institutions, and community-based organizations to become more involved in the lives of troubled young people. According to Michael P. Brown, these groups can teach values to young people and get them started on their paths toward fulfilling careers.

Also, intervention programs should engage cities and towns to promote delinquency prevention programs. Programs should also be established to support families. Says Brown, "Parents are primarily responsible for instilling in their children socially redeeming morals and values. Parenting classes may be necessary when mothers and or fathers lack the skills, abilities, and maturity to socialize their offspring properly."[80]

## Waiting for the Answer

As community leaders, judges, and other officials struggle with the problem of juvenile delinquency, they are well aware that juvenile crime has been a problem for Americans dating back to the colonial era. Despite the reforms of the twentieth and twenty-first centuries, in which new laws and new strategies were employed to deal with young offenders, the problem of juvenile delinquency has never gone away.

New evidence has shown that young offenders may not be entirely at fault—that because their brains are still developing, many delinquents simply do not realize the consequences of their actions. In the case of Omer Ninham and Richard Crapeau, they were well aware that they would hurt and perhaps kill Zong Vang when they hurled him off the roof of a parking garage, but they might not have understood that their brief act of cruelty could cause them to lose their freedom for the rest of their lives.

And so defendants like Ninham and Crapeau find themselves in a system enmeshed in the throes of a great debate. On the one hand, some advocates call for young offenders to be treated as adults and punished with long imprisonments. In contrast, many advocates insist that young people should be given a chance for rehabilitation and starting anew. As this debate continues, many young people will likely spend long hours in prison, waiting for society to find the answer.

# Facts

- The Oregon Youth Authority, which administers the state's juvenile detention programs, reported in 2011 that 71 percent of offenders who obtain high school diplomas while in the agency's custody go on to lead crime-free lives.

- A 2008 Indiana study found that adult and juvenile prisons have less success in rehabilitating young offenders than group homes and similar programs: About a third of juveniles released from Indiana prisons are incarcerated again within three years of their release.

- Colorado officials closed the state's boot camp program in 2010 after studies indicated the recidivism rate for camp graduates was 51 percent—only 2 percent lower than the recidivism rate for juveniles who had served their sentences in adult prisons.

- After expanding a home-based program to include some juveniles convicted of felonies, Florida officials reported in 2010 that recidivism for those offenders dropped 31 percent. Those offenders would otherwise have served their sentences in detention centers.

- The 2011 study of juvenile offender recidivism in North Carolina found that 45 percent of offenders whose cases were dismissed by the court went on to commit additional crimes; meanwhile, 38 percent of juveniles who were diverted into community-based programs were also arrested again.

# Related Organizations and Websites

### American Bar Association (ABA)

321 N. Clark St.
Chicago, IL 60654-7598
phone: (800) 285-2221
website: www.americanbar.org

The ABA is the professional association of American attorneys. Visitors to the ABA website can download copies of the organization's three-part series *Dialogue on Youth and Justice,* which provides a history of juvenile justice in America, including the key cases decided by the US Supreme Court.

### American Civil Liberties Union (ACLU)

125 Broad St., 18th Floor
New York, NY 10004
phone: (212) 549-2500
website: www.aclu.org

The ACLU has represented juvenile offenders in challenging statutes that mandate they be tried in adult courts. By following the link to Juvenile Justice, visitors to the ACLU website can find updates on the Michigan cases in which the ACLU is challenging the state law that mandates life sentences to juveniles convicted in homicide cases.

## Campaign for Youth Justice (CFYJ)

1012 Fourteenth St. NW
Washington, DC 20005
phone: (202) 558-3580
fax: (202) 386-9807
e-mail: info@cfyj.org
website: www.campaignforyouthjustice.org

This advocacy group is dedicated to ending laws that enable prosecutors to try juvenile offenders in adult courts. Visitors to the organization's website can find the report *Jailing Juveniles*. Numerous young offenders and their parents also provide their own stories on the website.

## Center for Juvenile Justice Reform (CJJR)

Georgetown University
3300 Whitehaven St. NW, Suite 5000
Washington, DC 20057-1485
phone: (202) 687-7657
fax (202) 687-3110
website: http://cjjr.georgetown.edu

Headquartered at Georgetown University, the CJJR researches trends in juvenile justice. Visitors to the center's website can find many news articles reporting on the dangers and drawbacks of trying juveniles in adult courtrooms.

## Citizens Against Homicide (CAH)

336 Bon Air Center
Greenbrae, CA 94904
phone: (415) 455-5944
fax: (415) 721-0788
e-mail: vctmsmurdr@aol.com
website: www.citizensagainsthomicide.org

This nonprofit advocacy group supports families of homicide victims. The organization has initiated campaigns to keep juvenile offenders in prison and lobbies against adoption of laws that would permit paroles for juveniles convicted in homicide cases.

## Death Penalty Information Center (DPIC)

1015 Eighteenth St. NW, 704
Washington, DC 20036
phone: (202) 289-2275
fax: (202) 289-7336
website: www.deathpenaltyinfo.org

The nonprofit group collects facts about the death penalty in America. The organization's website maintains a database of the juvenile offenders who were executed prior to the 2005 US Supreme Court decision that outlawed the death penalty for young defendants.

## Equal Justice Initiative (EJI)

122 Commerce St.
Montgomery, AL 36104
phone: (334) 269-1803
fax: (334) 269-1806
e-mail: contact_us@eji.org
website: www.eji.org

This nonprofit group provides free legal representation to defendants the organization believes have been denied fair justice. Among EJI's clients are young people who face life in prison. Visitors to the EJI website can follow the link to Children in Adult Prisons to find updates on the organization's cases.

## Human Rights Watch

350 Fifth Ave., 34th Floor
New York, NY 10118-3299
phone : (212) 290-4700
fax: (212) 736-1300
website: www.hrw.org

This international human rights group crusades to end the death penalty for juveniles in Iran, Saudi Arabia, and Sudan. Visitors to the organization's website can download the report *The Last Holdouts*, which chronicles the legal treatment of juveniles as adults in foreign countries and the harsh penalties they face, including the death penalty.

## Juvenile Law Center (JLC)

The Philadelphia Bldg., 4th floor
1315 Walnut St
Philadelphia, PA 19107
phone (800) 875-8887
fax: (215) 625-2808
website: www.jlc.org

This nonprofit group advocates for the rights of juvenile defendants. Visitors to the group's website can find many publications, fact sheets, and statistics chronicling the treatment of juveniles in the American justice system.

## National Council on Crime and Delinquency (NCCD)

1970 Broadway, Suite 500
Oakland, CA 94612
phone: (510) 208-0500
fax: (510) 208-0511
e-mail: info@sf.nccd-crc.org
website: www.nccd-crc.org

The council studies trends in juvenile crime and drafts strategies for governments and communities to address the problem. Students can follow the link on the council's website to Publications, where they can find reports on such topics as wilderness camps and girls in juvenile justice.

## National Juvenile Justice Network (NJJN)

1710 Rhode Island Ave. NW, 10th Floor
Washington, DC 20036
phone (202) 467-0864
fax (202) 887-0738
e-mail: info@njjn.org
website: www.njjn.org

The NJJN lobbies against incarceration of young offenders in adult prisons, supporting instead community-based intervention systems to divert juveniles from crime. Visitors to the NJJN website can find many resources, including several articles reporting on the scientific research proving that the adolescent brain is still developing.

### National Organization of Victims of Juvenile Lifers (NOVJL)

PO Box 498
Davisburg, MI 48350
phone: (847) 446-7073
e-mail: NOVJL@aol.com
website: www.teenkillers.org

This advocacy group lobbies for tougher sentences for violent juvenile offenders. Visitors to the organization's website can find many stories of young offenders who committed murders after they were released from custody. The website also includes updates on campaigns to toughen juvenile sentencing laws in several states.

### US Office of Juvenile Justice and Delinquency Prevention (OJJDP)

810 Seventh St. NW
Washington, DC 20531
phone: (202) 307-5911
website: www.ojjdp.gov

An agency of the US Department of Justice, OJJDP performs studies of juvenile delinquency, as well as conducting intervention, rehabilitation, and detention programs. Visitors to the agency's website can download copies of *Juvenile Offenders and Victims*, the national report on juvenile crime that is updated periodically.

# Additional Reading

## Books

Thomas J. Bernard and Megan C. Kurlychek, *The Cycle of Juvenile Justice*. New York: Oxford University Press, 2010.

William J. Chambliss, ed., *Juvenile Crime and Justice*. Thousand Oaks, CA: Sage, 2011.

David Chura, *I Don't Wish Nobody to Have a Life Like Mine: Tales of Kids in Adult Lockup*. Boston: Beacon, 2011.

Nancy Dowd, ed., *Justice for Kids: Keeping Kids Out of the Juvenile Justice System*. New York: New York University Press, 2011.

Irene Sullivan, *Raised by the Courts: One Judge's Insight into Juvenile Justice*. New York: Kaplan, 2010.

## Periodicals

James C. Backstrom, "America's Juvenile Justice System Is Not Broken," *Prosecutor*, January/March 2008.

Jess Bravin, "Justices Restrict Life Terms for Youths," *Wall Street Journal*, May 18, 2010.

Karen Heller, "Life Terms for Juveniles? Pennsylvania Is the US Leader in Jailing Young People Without Any Hope of Parole," *Philadelphia Inquirer*, July 18, 2010.

Debra Bradley Ruder, "The Teen Brain: A Work in Progress," *Harvard Magazine*, September/October 2008.

Mosi Secret, "States Prosecute Fewer Teenagers in Adult Courts," *New York Times*, March 6, 2011.

# Internet Sources

International Justice Project, Background—"The Constitutionality of the Juvenile Death Penalty." www.internationaljustice project.org/juvConst.cfm.

Kids and Crime, "In Re Gault, 30 Years Later." www.kidsand crime.com/?p=5.

PBS.com, *Inside the Teenage Brain.* www.pbs.org/wgbh/pages /frontline/shows/teenbrain.

PBS.com, *Juvenile Justice: Should Teens Who Commit Serious Crimes Be Tried as Children or Adults?,* www.pbs.org/wgbh/pages/front line/shows/juvenile.

*Pittsburgh Post-Gazette*, "Is This Justice?," www.post-gazette.com /regionstate/20010318jintro0318areg2.asp.

# Source Notes

## Introduction: When Young People Face Life in Prison

1. Quoted in Todd Richmond, Associated Press, "Cruel-Punishment Plea Fails," *Philadelphia Inquirer*, May 21, 2011, p. A2.

2. Human Rights Watch, *The Rest of Their Lives: Life Without Parole for Child Offenders*, October 11, 2005. www.hrw.org.

3. Quoted in National Juvenile Justice Network, *Polling on Public Attitudes About the Treatment of Young Offenders*, June 2010. http://njjn.org.

4. National Organization of Victims of Juvenile Lifers, "The Public Policy Debate About Juvenile Life Without Parole," June 2011. www.teenkillers.org.

5. Shay Bilchik, "Juvenile Delinquency Prevention," testimony before the US Senate Judiciary Committee, December 5, 2007.

6. Quoted in Richmond, "Cruel-Punishment Plea Fails," p. A2.

## Chapter One: What Are the Roots of the Juvenile Offender Controversy?

7. David N. Sandberg, "Resolving the Gault Dilemma," *New Hampshire Bar Journal*, Summer 2007. www.nhbar.org.

8. Quoted in Anthony M. Platt, *The Child Savers: The Invention of Delinquency*. Chicago: University of Chicago Press, 1977, p. 161.

9. Quoted in History of the Supreme Court, "In Re: Gault," May 15, 1967. www.historyofsupremecourt.org.

10. Michael P. Brown, "Juvenile Offenders: Should They Be Tried in Adult Courts?," *USA Today Magazine*, January 1998, p. 52.

11. US Supreme Court Center, "*McKeiver vs. Pennsylvania*," June 21, 1971. http://supreme.justia.com.

12. Brown, "Juvenile Offenders," p. 52.

13. Quoted in *Frontline*, "Juvenile Justice," January 30, 2001. www.pbs.org.

14. Quoted in Barbara White Stack, "Is This Justice? A Reform Movement Crumbles," *Pittsburgh Post-Gazette*, March 19, 2001. www.post-gazette.com.

## Chapter Two: Are Juveniles Responsible for the Crimes They Commit?

15. Quoted in Kathleen Parrish, "Gumbs' Parents Apologize to Ice Victim's Kin," *Allentown (PA) Morning Call*, August 6, 2003. http://articles.mcall.com.

16. Quoted in Christine Schiavo, "Fatal Ice-Tossing Case Sent to Juvenile Court," *Philadelphia Inquirer*, June 24, 2003. http://articles.philly.com.

17. Quoted in Brian Callaway, "Ice-Chunk Death Defendant Freed," *Allentown (PA) Morning Call*, May 14, 2008. http://articles.mcall.com.

18. Quoted in Callaway, "Ice-Chunk Death Defendant Freed."

19. Quoted in CBS News, "Teens' Brains Key to Their Impulsiveness," February 11, 2009. www.cbsnews.com.

20. Richard G. Singer and John Q. La Fond, *Criminal Law: Examples and Explanations*. Austin, TX: Wolters Kluwer, 2010, p. 532.

21. Steven J. Berkowitz, "Child Prisoners: An Offense to Human Rights and Medical Ethics," Connecticut Juvenile Justice Alliance, January 2010. www.raisetheagect.org.

22. Governor's Juvenile Justice Commission, "Statement Related to Wisconsin's Age of Adult Criminal Responsibility," 2010. http://oja.state.wi.us.

23. Quoted in Richard Knox, "The Teen Brain: It's Just Not Grown Up Yet," National Public Radio, March 1, 2010. www.npr.org.

24. Quoted in Shannon Brownlee et al. "Inside the Teen Brain," *US News & World Report*, August 9, 1999, p. 44.

25. Quoted in Tara Parker-Pope, "Teenagers, Friends and Bad Decisions," *New York Times*, February 3, 2011. http://well.blogs.nytimes.com.

26. Quoted in Knox, "The Teen Brain: It's Just Not Grown Up Yet."

27. Robert Epstein, "The Myth of the Teen Brain," *Scientific American Special Edition: Childhood Development*, June 2007, p. 68.

28. Quoted in Julia Reynolds, "Crime and the Teenage Brain," *Monterey (CA) Herald*, October 7, 2007. www.montereyherald.com.

29. Quoted in Joline Gutierrez Krueger, "Brain Science Offers Insight to Teen Crime," *Albuquerque Tribune*, December 8, 2006. www.abqtrib.com.

## Chapter Three: Do Adult Court Sentences Deter Juvenile Crime?

30. Kenneth Sukhia, testimony before the US House Subcommittee on Crime, House Judiciary Committee, March 11, 1999. http://judiciary.house.gov.

31. Sukhia, testimony.

32. Brown, "Juvenile Offenders," p. 52.

33. Quoted in Chris Togneri, "Twelve-Year-Old Could Become Pennsylvania Prison's Youngest Inmate Ever," *Pittsburgh Tribune-Review*, June 12, 2010. www.pittsburghlive.com.

34. Quoted in Paul Peirce, "Prison with Principle," *Pittsburgh Tribune-Review*, December 26, 2004. www.pittsburghlive.com.

35. Quoted in Peirce, "Prison with Principle."

36. Quoted in Togneri, "Twelve-Year-Old Could Become Pennsylvania Prison's Youngest Inmate Ever."

37. Quoted in Ovetta Wiggins, "At Newest Pennsylvania Prison, Juveniles Come of Age," *Philadelphia Inquirer*, April 2, 2001. http://articles.philly.com.

38. Quoted in Wiggins, "At Newest Pennsylvania Prison, Juveniles Come of Age."

39. Quoted in Marilyn Elias, "Is Adult Prison Best for Juveniles?," *USA Today*, September 20, 2006. www.usatoday.com.

40. Quoted in *Syracuse (NY) Post-Standard*, "More New York Juvenile Offenders Moved to Adult Prisons Last Year than in Previous Five Years," March 17, 2011. http://blog.syracuse.com.

41. T.J. Parsell, "Unsafe Behind Bars," *New York Times*, September 18, 2005, p. LI-17.

42. Campaign for Youth Justice, *Jailing Juveniles*, November 2007, p. 7. www.campaignforyouthjustice.org.

43. Campaign for Youth Justice, *Jailing Juveniles*, pp. 7–8.

44. Quoted in Campaign for Youth Justice, *Jailing Juveniles*, p. 11.

45. Richard E. Redding, *Juvenile Transfer Laws: An Effective Deterrent to Delinquency?,* US Department of Justice Office of Justice Programs, June 2010. www.ncjrs.gov.

46. Quoted in Bryan Robinson, "2 Teens at Center of Juvenile Crime Debate," ABC News, March 9, 2001. http://abcnews.go.com.

47. Quoted in Wiggins, "At Newest Pennsylvania Prison, Juveniles Come of Age."

48. James C. Backstrom, "America's Juvenile Justice System Is Not Broken," *Prosecutor*, January/March 2008, p. 12.

## Chapter Four: Should Juvenile Offenders Face the Death Penalty?

49. Quoted in International Justice Project, "Scott Hain: Juvenile Offender in Oklahoma," 2003. www.internationaljusticeproject.org.

50. John Laurence, "The Earliest Practices of the Death Penalty," in *The Complete History of the Death Penalty*, ed. Hayley R. Mitchell. San Diego: Greenhaven, 2001, p. 67.

51. Quoted in Holly Brewer, *By Birth or Consent: Children, Law, and the Anglo-American Revolution in Authority.* Chapel Hill: University of North Carolina Press, 2005, p. 222.

52. Quoted in Lynn Cothern, *Juveniles and the Death Penalty.* Washington, DC: Coordinating Council on Juvenile Justice

and Delinquency Prevention, November 2000, p. 3. www
.ncjrs.gov.

53. Quoted in Anne James and Joanne Cecil, "Out of Step: Juvenile Death Penalty in the United States," *International Journal of Children's Rights*, July 2003, p. 292.

54. Sandra Day O'Connor, *Thompson v. Oklahoma*, June 29, 1988. www.law.cornell.edu.

55. Antonin Scalia, *Stanford v. Kentucky*, June 26, 1989. www.law.cornell.edu.

56. Quoted in James and Cecil, "Out of Step," p. 291.

57. Joan Jacobs Brumberg, "Separating the Killers from the Boys," *New York Times*, December 18, 2003, p. 43.

58. Quoted in Charles Lane, "5-4 Supreme Court Abolishes Juvenile Executions," *Washington Post*, March 2, 2005, p. A1.

59. Quoted in MSNBC, "Justices Abolish Death Penalty for Juveniles," March 1, 2005. www.msnbc.msn.com.

60. Quoted in MSNBC, "Justices Abolish Death Penalty for Juveniles."

61. Don Boys, "Should Teens Be Executed?," CST News, August 16, 2005. www.cstnews.com.

62. James Alan Fox, "Take Death Penalty off Table for Teen Murderers," *USA Today*, February 9, 2004, p. A17.

63. Quoted in Adam Liptak, "Justices Limit Life Sentences for Juveniles," *New York Times*, May 18, 2010, p. A1.

## Chapter Five: Can Juvenile Offenders Be Rehabilitated?

64. Quoted in Joseph P. Fried, "A Turnaround Born of Pain, Now Yielding Opportunity," *New York Times*, February 9, 2007, p. B6.

65. Quoted in Fried, "A Turnaround Born of Pain," p. B.6.

66. Quoted in Myron B. Pitts, "Youth Camps Were Tax Dollars Well Spent," *Fayetteville (NC) Observer*, April 14, 2011. www.fayobserver.com.

67. Quoted in Pitts, "Youth Camps Were Tax Dollars Well Spent."

68. Quoted in Mike Todd, "Youths Straighten Up at Boot Camp," *Austin American-Statesman*, March 29, 1996, p. B1.

69. Quoted in Sara Rimer, "States Adjust Adult Prisons to Needs of Youth Inmates," *New York Times*, July 25, 2001. www.ny times.com.

70. Quoted in Rimer, "States Adjust Adult Prisons to Needs of Youth Inmates."

71. Enrico Pagnanelli, "Children as Adults: The Transfer of Juveniles to Adult Courts and the Potential Impact of *Roper v. Simmons*," *American Criminal Law Review*, Winter 2007, p. 175.

72. Lonn Lanza-Kaduce, Charles E. Frazier, Jodi Lane, and Donna M. Bishop, *Juvenile Transfer to Criminal Court Study: Final Report*, Florida Department of Juvenile Justice, January 8, 2002, p. 25. www.prisonpolicy.org.

73. Quoted in Lanza-Kaduce et al., *Juvenile Transfer to Criminal Court Study: Final Report*, p. 38.

74. Quoted in Lanza-Kaduce et al., *Juvenile Transfer to Criminal Court Study: Final Report*, pp. 39–40.

75. Pagnanelli, "Children as Adults," p. 175.

76. Quoted in Lanza-Kaduce et al., *Juvenile Transfer to Criminal Court Study: Final Report*, p. 52.

77. Quoted in Lanza-Kaduce et al., *Juvenile Transfer to Criminal Court Study: Final Report*, p. 53.

78. Quoted in Lanza-Kaduce et al., *Juvenile Transfer to Criminal Court Study: Final Report*, p. 44.

79. Howard N. Snyder and Melissa Sickmund, *Juvenile Offenders and Victims: 2006 National Report*, National Center for Juvenile Justice, US Department of Justice, March 2006, p. 234. www.ncjjservehttp.org.

80. Brown, "Juvenile Offenders," p. 52.

# Index

# Picture Credits

# About the Author

Hal Marcovitz is a former journalist and the author of more than 150 books for young readers. As a news reporter, he spent more than a quarter-century covering courts and legal issues.